First published in Great Britain in 2018
by DC Thomson Media.
Meadowside,
Dundee,
Scotland
DD1 9QJ

Pass It On

Cooking Tips From The 1950s

Edited by Steve Finan

ISBN 978-1-84535-726-9

Dedication

For my mother, Elizabeth Finan,
1930-2012

The creator of the best "piece and dip"
ever eaten

Thanks to:

Gillian Martin
Jacqui Hunter
Sylwia Jackowska
Nikki Fleming
Deirdre Vincent
Sara Cunningham
Craig Houston
Denise West
Dawn Donaghey
Maggie Dun
Claire Johnston
Kay Burness
David Powell
Barry Sullivan
Duncan Laird
Fiona Brown
James Kirk
Fraser T. Ogilvie

And special thanks to cover model Nic Hutchison.

Introduction

TODAY, it is almost impossible to imagine how difficult it was to feed a family in the 1950s. The years until rationing finally ended, in 1954, were particularly taste-poor. There were no spices, few oils, and not much food to work with. Meat was roasted, vegetables were boiled and fruit was unsweetened. And that was when you could get your hands on beef, tatties and bananas.

The only things that were plentiful were scarcities.

Somehow, though, we survived. Somehow, mothers found ways to put out food that we look back on with nostalgic longing.

They were ingenious. They had to be. They found little secrets to make things taste better, or be just that little bit different. They were kitchen heroes.

And when they had a good idea, they shared it. They wrote to newspapers and magazines that would pay ten shillings for such gems of information, or even a guinea for the "tip of the week".

This book is a collection of those tips, gleaned from the best cooks who ever lived — your mother and grandmother.

They are taken mostly from The Sunday Post and People's Journal, newspapers which circulated widely in Scotland. The Post achieved saturation coverage every Sunday, up to 85% of Scottish adults read it. If your name was on its pages, then everyone knew about it. A golden light of housewifely prowess shone upon you.

These tips are drops of wisdom from the best of the best.

This was also the period of the recipes pamphlet. These were given away with magazines, with kitchen goods, flour, baking powder and even by various governmental bodies. They were then kept. Indeed, they were kept for years, even decades, tucked in a kitchen drawer or the back of a cupboard until they became sticky taped-together family heirlooms holding "that" recipe for scones, pancakes, or a variation on mince 'n' tatties.

This book is proud to reprint some of the "greats" from that selection of treasured scraps of paper, with their original publication date and author's name, wherever possible.

Ca' canny

THE tips, recipes and droplets of wisdom in this book are printed exactly as they appeared in the 1950s. They have not been tested or tasted, largely because I'm not brave enough to comment on or criticise my mother's, and her generation's, skills.

So if you follow their instructions but your scones are ruined, or your Sheep's Head Soup doesn't come out as expected, then blame them, not me.

The amounts of salt, vinegar, mustard (and sheep heads) recommended might also seem excessive to today's health-conscious society. Again, these recipes are from a different era, when salt and fat intake was seen in a different light.

The spellings, terminology and measurements have also been left untouched — you won't find a kilo or litre in here, but you will see gills, spoonfuls and quarter-ounces. You'll have to work out equivalent quantities for yourself. Good luck.

It has been, however, a joy and a privilege to work with this material. And I welcome the fact that the recipes might be a little salty, or a little sweet, by modern standards. I remain in awe of the skills and inventiveness of the wonderful, clever people who wrote in to newspapers and magazines with tips, or freely gave their treasured recipes.

No matter where these people are now, or how long ago they passed, I salute and fulsomely thank them.

Their wisdom deserves to live on.

Steve Finan, 2018.

Contents

Chapter 1

The Great 1950s Bake Off

TUNE in to any of the baking shows scattered across modern TV schedules like handfuls of flour and you find contestants, judges and experts referring to cakes, bread, scones and sponges "like mum used to make". They are trying to evoke the memories we all carry of the culinary expertise of our mother or grandmother....and hoping their cooking is as good.

You can forgive them, because we all have a fond attachment to a cake or scone recipe our mum used to make, don't we?

Everyone does.

There's a reason for that — whatever that recipe was, it truly was good. The high-water mark of British home baking was reached in the 1950s. Making your own cakes and scones was a necessity in those times of rationing (in the early '50s) and long before the days of supermarket shelves filled with every type of cake imaginable. It was also a matter of pride. Your mum made scones like no one else. Her scones were the best.

There was vast experience and many secrets — a drop of vanilla essence here, a special way to prepare the dough there. It is those snippets of expertise that are shared here. These tips are in those housewives' words. They are the ingredients and techniques of how they mixed, kneaded and baked your childhood.

February 5, 1950.
HOT TIP! — Cake tins don't need to be greased when you're baking large cakes, if you put the tins in the oven and make them really hot. The mixture should then be put into a hot tin and the tin returned to the oven. When turned out, the cakes have a smooth appearance, and aren't so apt to burn or stick. — **Miss M. L. Richardson, Duncarse, Dundee.**

March 5, 1950.
BANANA CREAM — Add a sliced banana to the white of an egg and beat until stiff. The banana disappears and you have a delicious substitute for whipped cream. — **Mrs Pettigrew, 7 Langholm Street, Scotstoun, Glasgow.**

March 5, 1950.
SWISS ROLLS — To prevent a Swiss roll from sticking to greased paper when ready, turn it out on to a clean cloth. Grease the paper at the sides then dip a tablespoon in water and rub the back of the spoon all over the top of the paper. The paper comes away quite cleanly. — **Mrs A. Thomson, 259 Blackness Road, Dundee.**

May 14, 1950.
NEW CAKE — New cake usually crumbles when cut with a knife. Use ordinary cotton thread as a cutter. Work the thread, saw fashion, through the cake. It will be a clean-cut job. — **Mrs Priestley, c/o 25 Ramsay Road, Kirkcaldy.**

July 16, 1950.
PASTRY CASES — Instead of filling small pastry tart cases with dried breadcrumbs or rice to stop them rising, turn the patty tins upside down and put pastry on the outside. When baked and taken off, the cases will be just right for filling. — **Mrs E.A. M. Gear, 2 Warehouse Flats, Woodgreen, Witney, Oxon.**

August 13, 1950.
FRUIT — If currants and raisins are scalded, drained and then tossed in flour, they are less likely to sink to the bottom in the baking of a rich cake. — **Mrs J. Nicol, Gordondale, Port Elphinstone, Inverurie.**

October 22, 1950.
BAKING — When baking a large cake, set your alarm clock at the time it should be cooked. If your duties take you to another part of the house, the alarm will bring you back to your cooker and cake. — **Mrs E. Muers, 19 Cecil Street, Sunderland.**

Table talk

AN Apple a day

One of the nicest—and simplest recipes for a hot sweet is Everton Apples. Pare and core 4 medium sized cooking apples, and stuff them with brown sugar and butter. Place in baking tin with 3 tablespoonful water. Cover and bake in moderate oven till tender. Serve hot with custard made with Brown & Polson Custard Powder.

Tinned Fruit a la Ritz

Here's a way to serve tinned peaches, pears or apricots. Drain the fruit and place in deep dish. Mix 3 level dessertspoons Brown & Polson 'Patent' Cornflour with a little cold milk. Put rest of pint on to heat with 1 tablespoonful sugar, nut of butter, pinch of salt. Add mixed cornflour, stir till boiling, boil for 3 minutes. Stir in 3 tablespoonsful desiccated coconut. Pour over fruit and leave to cool. Serve with the fruit juice thickened with a little cornflour.

KEEP YOUR MERINGUES

Shapely

Be sure to add a little Brown & Polson 'Patent' Cornflour with the sugar. For best results, use 2 oz. sugar and 1 teaspoonful cornflour to each egg white.

MAKE THESE

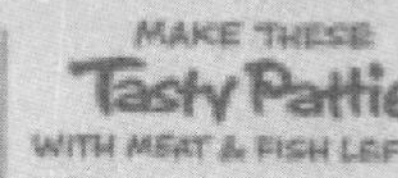

WITH MEAT & FISH LEFTOVERS

First make a smooth white sauce with 3 teaspoonsful Brown & Polson 'Patent' Cornflour, nut of butter and 1 pint milk. (You'll find full instructions on the 'Patent' Cornflour packet.) Season well, then mix in the chopped oddments of meat or fish. Fill the baked pastry cases and serve hot.

new

in milk puddings

Raisin and Caramel Pudding is made in a matter of minutes, and can be eaten hot or cold. Take the contents of the Caramel envelope in the 5-flavour packet of Brown & Polson Flavoured Cornflour, and make a pudding as directed on the packet. Swell some raisins (or sultanas) in boiling water, drain and stir into the pudding while it is still cooking.

For EXTRA Lightness

In steamed and baked sponge puddings, replace 1 tablespoonful of the flour in your recipe with 1 tablespoonful Brown & Polson 'Patent' Cornflour. They'll have a lovely melt-in-the-mouth texture.

It's made for enjoyment when it's made with

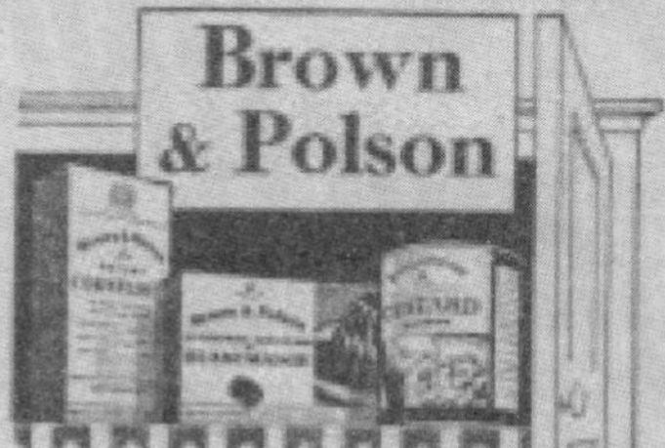

'PATENT' CORNFLOUR ★ FLAVOURED CORNFLOUR FOR BLANCMANGE
CUSTARD POWDER

BY APPOINTMENT CORNFLOUR MANUFACTURERS TO THE LATE KING GEORGE VI. BROWN & POLSON LIMITED, PAISLEY, SCOTLAND

December 31, 1950.
FRESH CAKE — When cutting a cake, first cut in two, then cut the slices from the centre and push the two remaining pieces close together like a whole cake. The cake will then keep moist and soft. **— Mrs R. Dick, 25 Chirnside Road, Glasgow.**

January 7, 1951.
NEW CAKE TINS — Always bake new cake tins in the oven until discoloured before using them. They absorb the heat better and cook well underneath. A shiny cake tin baffles heat. — **Miss L. Wilkie, 33 Sciennes Road, Edinburgh.**

January 21, 1951.
QUICK COOKING — A cake takes less time to bake if a small, earthenware jam jar is greased and put in the centre of the tin before you add the mixture. — **Mrs McGrath, Holyoake, Hurlford, Kilmarnock.**

April 1, 1951.
CAKE RESCUE — When a cake sticks to the tin, stand it over a bowl of boiling water. The heat loosens the cake. — **Mrs J. Hill, 53 Calder Street, Alloa.**

July 29, 1951.
PASTRY — When making pastry, instead of using the usual wooden rolling pin, fill a glass bottle with cold water. You'll improve the texture. — **Mrs Elizabeth L. Thomson, 82 Main Street, Cumbernauld, by Glasgow.**

December 30, 1951.
DRY CAKE — Fruit cake that has been baked too long and is rather dry can be moistened by pouring a little sherry into holes made with a skewer. Leave for a little time, and you'll find the flavour much improved. — **Mrs J. M. MacKenzie, 7 Davaar Avenue, Campbeltown, Argyll.**

March 9, 1952.
RICH CAKE — Unable to get dried fruit for baking, I used half a jar of mincemeat to add to my usual sultana cake mixture. Result — a rich cake with time saved in cleaning fruit beforehand. — **Margaret Hudson, 11 Minto Street, Glasgow.**

April 13, 1952.
BEATING — When mixing and beating, place the baking bowl on a damp, rumpled pad of wet cloth. This gives the bowl a firm grip. — **Mrs E. W. McNeill, 71 Finnart Street, Greenock.**

August 31, 1952.
SCONES — Always mix dough for scones with a knife, cutting through the dough as you mix. Don't handle the mixture much and you'll have lighter scones. — **Mrs C. Munro, 104 Bothwell Street, Glasgow.**

October 19, 1952.
OVER-COOKED — If a fruit cake has been over-cooked on top, scrape the burnt part off, brush over with beaten white of egg, dust with castor sugar and replace in oven for a few minutes. — **Mrs J. Scott, Hairmuir, Benholm, Montrose.**

November 23, 1952.
CAKE MAKING — If your butter and sugar for a cake goes oily, stand it in a basin of cold water for 15 to 20 minutes. You'll find it creams quite easily. — **Mrs J. D. Hildreth, 13 Dean Road, Norton Malton, Yorks.**

December 14, 1952.
CANDIED PEEL — Instead of tediously cutting up candied peel with a knife, rub it on the suet grater. Fine, even slices will result, and much time saved. — **Miss Cattenach, Craiglea, Newtonmore.**

February 1, 1953.
PASTRY — When making pastry, add a dessertspoonful of semolina to each 1lb. of flour. The result is a lovely short crust and no sticking to pastry board or rolling pin. — **Mrs C. B. Ross, 80 Beaufort Gardens, Bishopbriggs, Glasgow.**

FOOD NEWS **March 15, 1953.**

FRUITIER CAKE – AND MORE OF IT – BY OUR FOOD REPORTER

BAKERS are being given 20 per cent. more dried fruit from next Sunday. So fruitier cake will soon be on sale in bigger quantities. And housewives will be pleased that this time their bigger dried fruit allocation will be mostly Californian seedless raisins.

March 22, 1953.
CAKE HINT — To prevent a cake being overfired on top, run cold water tap over buttered greaseproof paper. Shake well and place over cake before putting it in oven. — **Miss J. Dobbie, 1 Auld Castle Road, Inverness.**

May 31, 1953.
EASY MIXING — When mixing custard powders and gravy thickeners, add dry ingredients a little at a time to the liquid instead of the other way round. This makes mixing easier and gives smoother paste. — **Mrs W. Inglis, 6 Wharf Street, Montrose.**

August 9,1953.
NEW CAKE — I wanted to use a newly-baked and iced cake in a hurry. So I put it in the refrigerator for two hours. It was then ready for cutting. — **Mrs J. Oliver, 119 Evans Street, Larbert.**

November 29, 1953.
FLUFFY SCONES — Don't throw out a junket which hasn't set. Mix it with self-raising flour and make into scones. When baked, they're beautifully light and spongy. — **Mrs E. Deas, 20 Mossbank, Cowdenbeath.**

March 21, 1954.
CAKE-MAKING — When making a cake, put the tin in a warm oven for a few seconds before dropping in the cake mixture. Then there's no fear of the cake being heavy or sinking in the middle. — **Mrs A. Bird, St. Anne's, 101 Westcliff Park Drive, Westcliff-on-Sea.**

May 2, 1954.
FLAN CASES — When making cases for flans, turn baking tin upside down, grease and cover with pastry. This keeps the pastry a good shape and does away with rice, &c., for fillings. — **Mrs A. S. Peacock, 4 Highfield Road, Grove Hill, Middlesbrough.**

November 14, 1954.
WHEN BAKING — Keep a moist rubber sponge on the kitchen worktable when baking or cooking. It is handy to wipe sticky fingers on. — **Mrs M.J. Boswell, 12 Peter Street, Workington, Cumberland.**

January 16, 1955.
PASTRY — When making pastry, add a dessertspoonful of semolina to each 1lb. of flour. The result is a lovely short crust — and no sticking to pastry board or rolling pin. — **H. Parker, 6 Bowman Flat, Larkhall.**

March 6, 1955.
SMALL CAKES — When baking cakes in paper cases, place a small dish filled with water at the bottom of the oven, below the jets. This stops discoloration of the cases. — **Mrs I. Neish, 31 Holburne Place, Menstrie.**

April 3, 1955.
BISCUIT SHAPES — To make a variety of shapes when baking, release the crinkle-edged part of a round biscuit cutter, and you can press it into various shapes. — **J. Farquhar, 52 Auchmill Road, Bucksburn.**

Orange Bread

Fresh, tangy tea-time treat

Your family will be thrilled with this recipe. It's something new and different—but it's quite easy to make.

Sieve 8 oz. plain flour and 2 level teasp. Royal Baking Powder (twice). Then add 4 oz. sugar, 1 tablesp. marmalade, grated rind 1 orange, 1 tablesp. melted butter or margarine, 1 egg, and beat to dropping consistency with just under ¼ pint milk and water.

Pour mixture into a greased 1 lb. loaf tin and bake in a hot oven (Gas No. 6—400°F.) for 40-45 mins. The gentle, continuous raising action of Royal Baking Powder starts from the moment of mixing and continues right through until the bread is cooked, making it light and even textured. When baked through, turn bread out on to rack to cool. Eat in slices, plain or buttered.

Good cooks always recommend using plain flour and Baking Powder because different recipes need different amounts of raising agent. Using *just the right amount* of Royal Baking Powder with plain flour ensures perfect results for all your baking—pies, puddings and cakes. Royal Baking Powder is in small, medium and large tins, prices 1/3, 2/3, 4/1.

FREE: *For new revised cookery book "Baking with Sally" write to Dept. P, Standard Brands, Liverpool* **9.**

April 17, 1955.

PANCAKES — When turning pancakes on a hotplate, dip the knife in cold water. This prevents them sticking to knife, and does the job quicker. — **Miss I. Mackay, Holborn View, Thurso.**

May 15, 1955.
EASY TO SEE — Use a grater for pricking biscuits quickly and neatly. Roll out the dough, run the coarse part of a round grater over it firmly, and cut the dough in the usual way. — **M. Whiteside, 83 Aitkenhead Avenue, Coatbridge.**

May 22, 1955.
NO OVER-FLAVOURING — Keep a medicine dropper in the kitchen cupboard, and use it for measuring flavouring essences. There's no chance of over-flavouring. — **Miss E. Muers, 19 Cecil Street, Sunderland.**

September 4, 1955.
JAM ROLL — To prevent a jam roll from cracking when it's rolled up, turn it out on to a linen towel which has been wrung out in cold water. Roll the sponge up into the towel and leave it for a moment or two. You will find that the roll stays in perfect shape. — **Mrs Stenhouse, 27 Haliburton Road, Galashiels.**

September 11, 1955.
CAKE DECORATION — Shake up some desiccated coconut in a jar to which you've added a few drops of colouring. You can vary the depth of colour according to the amount of drops. Shake well until coconut is an even colour throughout. — **Mrs E. Stuart, 231 Cornhill Street, Glasgow.**

January 22, 1956.
BAKING HINT — I find it excellent to use a torch when looking into the oven to check the progress of baking. The contents can be clearly seen, and the door need only be opened a chink. — **Miss M. M. Birrell, 96 Kinnell Avenue, Glasgow.**

March 4, 1956.
CRISPS UP — If the bottom of an apple cake is too soft, slip it on to a warm, dry frying-pan for five minutes to firm. — **Miss M. Brown, 414 Edinburgh Road, Glasgow.**

April 29, 1956.
BAKING TIP — Milk should be used at room temperature to get the best results in baked products such as cakes, muffins, and biscuits. This is particularly important when melted shortening is used. — **Mrs Marshall, 30 Staffa Street, Glasgow.**

July 15, 1956.
GOOD SUBSTITUTE — Finding I had no greaseproof paper to line a cake tin, I split open a white paper bag, rubbed both sides with margarine, and it did the job perfectly. — **Mrs M. Younie, 425 Clifton Road, Aberdeen.**

December 9, 1956.
CAKE WITHOUT PEEL — For those who don't like peel in cake, use a large tablespoonful of orange marmalade. This gives the desired flavour without the hard pieces of peel. — **Mrs M. Murray, 17 Strathblane Road, Milngavie.**

December 23, 1956.
PERFECT CAKE — If your cake tin hasn't got a loose bottom, before lining the tin, fold a strip of greaseproof paper about six thicknesses and 2 inches wide. Put across centre of tin, leaving about 2 inches hanging over the edges. When cake is baked, this enables you to lift it out without any fear of breaking it. — **Mrs C. Jackson, 14 Linwood Grove, Darlington.**

January 27, 1957.
SCONES — If you like your oven scones nice and crisp on the bottom, grease the oven tray well before putting scones in oven. If you like them soft, sprinkle the oven tray with flour. — **J. Caldwell, 10 Murray Place, St Andrews.**

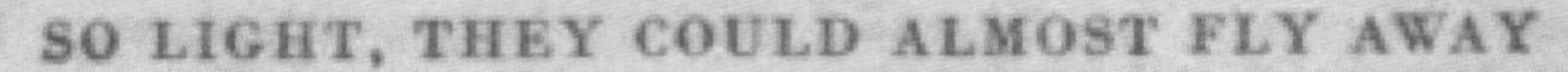

February 17, 1957.

MARZIPAN — When making marzipan, it is more economical to use ground mixed nuts, costing only about half the price of ground almonds. — **Mrs G. D. Haggart, 5 Windhill Place, Glasgow.**

March 3, 1957.

MERINGUES — When making meringues, put spoonfuls of the mixture on upturned patty cake tins. They come out of the oven with a ready-made hollow for the filling. — **Miss H. Wilson, 924 Tollcross Road, Glasgow.**

March 31, 1957.
BROWNING — To ensure perfect browning when firing a cake, make sure your browning sheet is well polished with steel wool. **— M. Nisbet, 220 Liberton Street, Glasgow.**

November 24, 1957.
WHEN BAKING — While heating the oven previous to baking, pop in all baking-tins, trays, &c., you are to use. It then takes very little time and fat to grease them. — **Mrs S. McArthur, 46 Cartside Road. Busby.**

December 8, 1957.
BUTTER CREAMING — If butter or margarine has to be softened quickly for creaming, place in a greaseproof paper inside a polythene bag. Tie tightly and drop in warm (not hot) water for a few minutes. — **Mrs E. M. Stark, 10 Park Avenue, Stirling.**

December 8, 1957.
FLOUR — Instead of sieving flour, &c., I find it much quicker, and equally satisfactory, to whisk it for a few seconds with a rotary beater. — **M.S. Cameron, 11 Dougalston Avenue, Milngavie.**

December 15, 1957.
BLACK BUN — When making black bun, place the fruit into a colander and then steam over a pan of boiling water for ten minutes. The flavour and appearance of the bun is greatly improved. — **Mrs D. Hamilton, 25 Whinneyknowe, North Queensferry.**

December 29, 1957.
PREVENTS BURNING — When baking large cakes, wrap a double layer of brown paper (or greaseproof paper) round the outside of the cake tin. Tie on with a piece of string. This keeps the cake from burning and it comes out a nice golden brown. — **Mrs A. Armstrong, Easington Demense, Belford.**

March 9, 1958.
FOR BATTER — Mix batter for pancakes and Yorkshire puddings in a large jug. Pour batter straight into a pan or tin without any mess. — **E. J. Jacques, 19 Berwick Road, Felpburn, Bognor Regis.**

June 29, 1958.
USE ICING — When making curds, I prefer to use icing sugar. It melts much more quickly. — **A. Anderson, 14 Ivanhoe Terrace, Hawick.**

July 6, 1958.
MERINGUES — When making meringues, try cooking them in bun tins turned upside down. Just put a spoonful of the mixture in each tin. They emerge beautifully from the oven, with a ready-made dent for the cream filling at the base of each meringue. — **Mrs P. Morgan, 10 Coronation Avenue, Tow Law, County Durham.**

July 27, 1958.
ANGEL CAKES — When making angel cakes, use a grapefruit knife to scoop out the top. You get a much tidier finish. — **Miss Picton, 80 Watson Street, Dundee.**

April 13, 1958.
UNUSUAL FILLING — Here's an unusual filling for a sandwich cake — a layer of peanut butter covered by a layer of orange marmalade. If desired, the cake may be topped with orange icing, but it is delicious without. — **Miss H. E. Sutherland, South View, Shap, Penrith.**

August 10, 1958.
BAKING TINS — When finished baking, rub baking sheets while still warm with greasy paper. This not only cleans them quickly, but prepares them for next baking day. — **Mrs J. Campbell, 18 Beech Avenue, Parkgate, Dumfries.**

August 24, 1958.

CUSTARD — A baked custard doesn't curdle if the dish is put into a tin of cold water before putting it in the oven. — **Mrs W. G. MacRae, 27 Spindlehowe Road, Uddingston, Glasgow.**

August 31, 1958.
TAKE A TIP — Place strips of greaseproof paper with ends sticking out at base of the sandwich tins. When ready, the sponges are easily removed. — **Mrs Joan Evans, 112 Albert Grove, Ruabon, Wrexham.**

November 16, 1958.
MACAROONS — When baking macaroons, sprinkle the top of the filling with caster sugar before putting in the oven. You then get a smooth professional finish. — **Mrs R. Stevenson, 14 Hermitage Crescent, Coatbridge.**

November 30, 1958.
BISCUITS — When making biscuits, roll out the mixture and instead of cutting with biscuit cutter, roll into a fat sausage. Roll in Demerara sugar. Then with a sharp knife cut off each biscuit. This method is a great time saver. — **Mrs McIntosh, Milltown, Ellon.**

December 21, 1958.
NO BROKEN EDGES — If you have difficulty in removing greaseproof paper from the bottom of your cake, heat it before the fire for a minute. It comes off easily. — **Mrs Meikle, 20 Meadow Park, Winchburgh.**

December 28, 1958.
LAYER CAKE — When making a layer cake which requires a soft filling, such as jelly, try putting a thin icing on the layers. Then spread the soft filling. It prevents the cake becoming soft and soggy. — **Mrs R. Davies, 167 Station Road, Lochgelly.**

January 25, 1959.
TRY IT! — When using custard for vanilla slices or custard puffs, stir into it, while hot, a dessertspoonful of gelatine. This ensures the custard doesn't become watery, as sometimes happens when it has been kept for a time. And the pastry remains nice and crisp.
— P. Scott, c/o 73 Almond Street, Grangemouth.

February 8, 1959.
VALENTINE CAKE — A pretty decoration for a Valentine cake is made from coloured fruit pastilles. Cut heart-shaped pieces and put round the edges of the iced cake. — **Mrs P. W. Morgan, 10 Coronation Avenue, Tow Law, Bishop Auckland.**

May 3, 1959.
CHERRY CAKE — When making a cherry cake, sift flour for cake in usual way. Put cherries in sieve beforehand. The result is that the cherries are perfectly floured and don't sink in the cake mixture. — **Mrs Jean Walker, 6 Dawson Street, Falkirk.**

May 10, 1959.
NO MORE BURNING — I found that my oven scones and cakes were always a bit burnt on the bottom no matter how well I lined my baking tray. I now line my tray with aluminium household foil and have no more burnt offerings. — **Mrs Brodie, 39 Barclay Street, Stonehaven.**

May 17, 1959.
SPONGE FLAN — Before filling a flan with fruit jelly, brush with melted margarine. This prevents the juices from making the sponge soggy. — **Mrs M. Riches, 34 Bexley Avenue, Newcastle.**

May 17, 1959.
DOUGHNUTS — One teaspoon of vinegar added to the fat in which doughnuts are fried prevents the cakes from absorbing the fat. — **Miss L. Sinclair, 35 Lorne Street, Edinburgh.**

May 17, 1959.
CAKE MAKING — After greasing a cake tin, put in a tablespoonful of breadcrumbs which have been dried in the oven. Shake them thoroughly all round the bottom and sides of the tin and tip out any which haven't stuck. When the cake is cooked it slips out without sticking. — **Mrs l. Waugh, 18 Wardlaw Street, Edinburgh.**

May 17, 1959.

GINGER CAKE — After preparing your cake mixture, grate preserved ginger into it. The ginger is then distributed evenly throughout. Cutting ginger into pieces is apt to make it sink to the bottom. — **Mrs A. H. Goodwin, 17 Beveridge Avenue, Glasgow.**

May 24, 1959.
NUT DECORATION — Before putting almonds on top of a cake, drop them in milk. They bake a pale brown and don't burn. — **Mrs E. W. Wallis, 9 Hillview Terrace, Edinburgh.**

June 7, 1959.
BAKING — When baking scones or crumpets on the hot-plate, instead of using fat try olive oil. It is cleaner and saves burnt fat smells in the kitchen. — **Mrs E. G. McGregor, Union Buildings, Turriff.**

June 21, 1959.
GINGER CAKE — If made with peanut butter instead of fat, ginger cake has a delicious nutty flavour. — **Mrs C. B. Ross, 80 Beaufort Gardens, Bishopbriggs, Glasgow.**

July 12, 1959.
BETTER FLAVOURING — When flavouring a sponge cake with orange or lemon rind, add the grated rind to the fat and sugar before creaming. This distributes the flavour more evenly through the cake. — **Mrs S. B. Guy, 121 Hirst Road, Harthill.**

August 2, 1959.
CHOCOLATE CAKE — I find that if I add the cocoa while creaming margarine and sugar it is evenly distributed and there will be no little black lumps in the finished cake. — **Mrs G. Temperley, 18 Backstone Road, Bridgehill, Blackhill, Co. Durham.**

September 6, 1959.
SPONGE CAKE — When making a sponge cake, separate the yolks from whites of eggs and whisk the whites stiff. Add yolks first in usual way, then fold in whites. This makes the sponge much lighter and fluffier. — **Mrs Joan Williamson, 41 Parkhead Avenue, Edinburgh.**

September 27, 1959.

MARSHMALLOWS — If marshmallows have become hard, put them in a polythene bag and dip into hot water. — **Miss R. Shepherd, Kalokeri, Silverknowes Road South, Edinburgh.**

October 18, 1959.
CAKE BAKING — When baking a cake, rub the wooden mixing spoon with margarine or butter beforehand. This prevents the mixture sticking to the spoon. – **Mrs Cruickshanks, 79 Stewart Crescent, Aberdeen.**

October 25, 1959.
BISCUITS — Use a grater for quickly and neatly pricking biscuits. Roll out dough, run the coarse part of a round grater over it firmly, and cut the dough in the usual way. — **Mrs B. Miller, 1 Pickering Road, Pennywell, Sunderland.**

October 25, 1959.
DOUGHNUTS — After frying doughnuts, roll them in sugar mixed with a little spice. This improves the flavour. — **Mrs C. Watkins, 114 Helensvale Street, Parkhead, Glasgow.**

November 22, 1959.
PANCAKES — When going to make pancakes the other day I found I was rather short of fresh milk. I had a tin of evaporated milk in the house, so I used it — one-third water to two-thirds milk. The pancakes were delicious and the evaporated milk was an improvement. — **Mrs Borland, 2001 Dumbarton Road, Glasgow.**

November 22, 1959.
CAKE TINS — To avoid lifting all the cake and biscuit tins from the cupboard to find the full one, replace the empty ones upside down. — **Miss Wendy Miller, Garscam Bungalow, Dalcroy, by Pitlochry.**

December 6, 1959.
CUSTARD — When making a baked egg custard, sprinkle some grated sponge crumbs in bottom of the dish. This prevents water forming in the custard. — **Miss W. A. Kettles, Roseisle, Montrose Road, Auchterarder.**

THOSE DOG-EARED OLD RECIPE PAMPHLETS...

A HIGH proportion of the pamphlets, scraps of paper and pages torn from books, that were kept in kitchen drawers and corners, were concerned with the greatly important matter of making the well-loved treats of the 1950s — scones, muffins, cakes, sponges, shortie and biscuits.

In other words, The Good Stuff!

These tips are drawn from a variety of sources. They have been taken from the original versions of what would become tatty, taped-together pages hoarded in your mother and grandmother's kitchen.

The identities of the cooks who drew up these recipes became lost in the flour-tinged mists of time, but the evidence of their expertise lived on.

These are tried, tested and tasted recipes. But they are more than that. When your mother, father, grandmother or aunt made these baked goods, they made them for you to enjoy. They made you smile. They cooked up the happy memories that you hold dear to this day.

They are evidence of motherly and family love displayed on a baking tray.

OVEN SCONES

8 oz. Flour
½ teaspoonful Bicarbonate of Soda
1½ oz. Margarine
1 teaspoonful Cream of Tartar
1 teaspoonful Milk
Castor Sugar
1 egg

Sift flour, salt, soda and cream of tartar.

Rub in the margarine lightly, add sugar, then mix to a soft, elastic dough with the unbeaten egg and a little milk.

Turn on to a floured board, and handling lightly, knead, then roll out to three-quarter-inch thickness.

Cut into rounds — a fluted cutter can be used, if wished — and place on a greased oven tray.

Bake in a quick oven (Regulo mark 7) for 10 to 15 minutes.

Currant Scones — Make as above, but add a tablespoonful and a half of currants to the dough before rolling out.

GIRDLE SCONES

1 teasponful Bicarbonate of Soda
2 teaspoonfuls Cream of Tartar
1 lb. Plain Flour
Pinch of Salt
Milk to mix

If sour or buttermilk is available, use this to mix scones, but add only one teaspoonful cream of tartar.

Sift flour and salt together, mix in the soda and cream of tartar, and form into a soft dough with milk.

Turn on to a floured board, knead very lightly and roll out to half-inch thickness. Cut into large rounds, cut each across in four and bake steadily on a hot girdle until well risen.

Turn and bake on the other side until quite dry in the centre. As scones are taken from the girdle, fold in a clean towel and allow to cool in this.

TREACLE SCONES

8 oz. Flour
1 teaspoonful Baking Powder
1½ oz. Margarine
½ teaspoonful Ground Ginger
1 oz. Castor Sugar
½ teaspoonful Cinnamon
Pinch of Salt
1 tablespoonful Treacle
Milk to mix

Rub margarine into the flour until fine, then mix in all dry ingredients. Warm treacle, mix with a little milk and add, making a fairly stiff dough.

Turn on to a floured board, knead lightly, and roll out to your desired size.

Place on a floured tin and bake in a moderate oven (Regulo mark 5) for about 20 minutes.

POTATO SCONES

½ lb. cold cooked Potatoes
½ oz. Margarine
2 oz. Flour
Good pinch of Salt
Milk

Mash potatoes with margarine and a very little milk, beating with a wooden spoon until light. Add the flour, sifted with the salt. Roll out on floured board very thinly, cut into rounds. Bake on a hot girdle for three minutes on each side. Cool on a towel.

CHOCOLATE MUFFINS

8 oz. Flour
Pinch of Salt
1½ oz. Chocolate Powder
1½ teaspoonfuls Baking Powder
3 oz. Margarine
2 Eggs
1½ gills Milk
3 oz. Sugar

Put milk and chocolate into saucepan and heat until chocolate is dissolved. Do not allow milk to boil. Sift flour with dry ingredients and stir in melted margarine, chocolate liquid and beaten eggs. Mix well together. Half-fill small, deep cake tins with the mixture — there will be about 14 muffins — and bake in a hot oven (Regulo mark 7) for about 20 minutes. Cool on a wire tray.

CHEESE MUFFINS

2 cupfuls Flour
8 teaspoonfuls Grated Cheese
4 teaspoonfuls Baking Powder
¾ cupful Milk
Good pinch of Salt

Sift together flour, baking powder and salt. Then mix in the cheese. Mix to a soft dough with the milk. Roll out lightly on floured board, cut into muffins and bake for 12 minutes in a hot oven (Regulo mark 7). This recipe makes about 14 muffins.

ONE-EGG SPONGE

5 oz. Self-Raising Flour
2½ oz. Margarine
2½ oz. Sugar
Milk
1 level teaspoonful Baking Powder
1 Egg

Simple and quick.

Sift flour with baking powder. Beat egg. Cream margarine and sugar until very light.

Add egg gradually, beating all the time, then fold in flour, adding rather less than a half a gill of milk. Put into greased tin and bake in a moderately hot oven (Regulo 5), allowing 20 to 25 minutes.

Allow to cool naturally.

SWISS ROLL

3 oz. Flour
¼ teaspoonful Baking Powder
3 Eggs
3½ oz. Castor Sugar
2 tablespoonfuls Jam

Prepare swiss roll tin or shallow baking tray by greasing and lining with paper. Put flour into oven to warm, then pass through sieve.

Break eggs into bowl, add sugar, and put over another basin of hot water. Beat until thick and frothy.

Take basin from heat and continue whisking until eggs are cool. Stir in the flour, adding the baking powder with the last spoonful. Pour into prepared tin and bake in a hot oven (Regulo 7) for 7 to 10 minutes.

Turn on to paper, dredged with castor sugar, spread with hot jam, and roll up.

CINNAMON BISCUITS

½ lb. Flour, ¼ lb., Margarine
1 Egg, ¼ lb. Castor Sugar
½ teaspoonful Baking Powder
1 teaspoonful Cinnamon
1 teaspoonful Mixed Spice

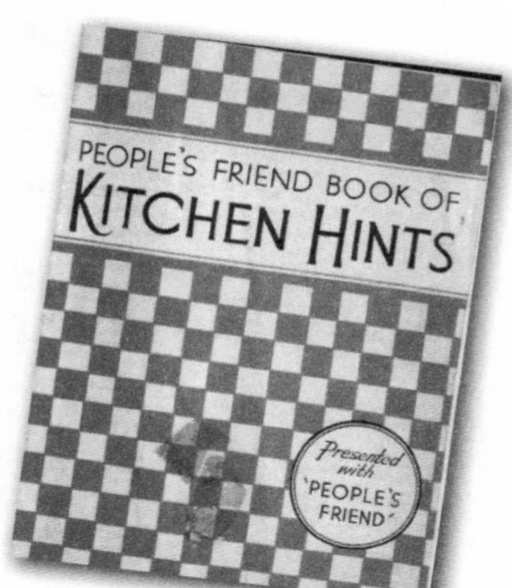

Biscuits are expensive to buy, but if you make them at home you can turn out a good number at small cost.

Here is a nice-tasted biscuit, and the recipe is very simple.

Beat the margarine and sugar to a cream, sift flour and spices together. Beat egg until creamy; add the flour, then the egg, to the creamed margarine and sugar.

Mix to a stiff dough, turn out on to a floured board, and work smoothly. Then roll out to ¼ inch thickness, cut into fancy shapes, lay on a greased and floured baking tray. Bake in a moderate oven for 15 to 20 minutes. Dredge with castor sugar while hot.

ALMOND BUNS

2 oz. Margarine
4 oz. Flour
2 oz. Currants
1 oz. Ground Almonds
2 oz. Castor Sugar
1 oz. Rice Flour
1 oz. Lemon Peel
1 Egg
½ teaspoonful Baking Powder

Sound good, don't they? Well, they taste as good, so give them a trial.

First thing to do is to cream butter and sugar, add rice flour and flour and baking powder, which have been previously well mixed. Stir in egg (well beaten), and lastly the currants, cleaned and picked, and the peel cut into small pieces, and ground almonds. Keep back a little of the almonds.

Form into small buns, sprinkle with the remainder of the almonds. Bake for about 15 minutes in a moderately hot oven.

COFFEE BUNS

¼ lb. Margarine
¼ lb. Demerara Sugar
½ lb. Self-Raising Flour
1 Egg
A few Currants
A little Milk

Fresh and fragrant from the oven, these little buns are very appetising. Cream the margarine and sugar till quite smooth, add the egg (well beaten), keeping a little back to brush over tops of buns. Add flour and a little milk to form into a stiff dough. Form into rounds about an inch thick; bake in a moderate oven for quarter of an hour. These quantities make about 14 buns.

COCONUT SQUARES

2 cupfuls Desiccated Coconut
2 Eggs
4 oz. Short Crust
2 cupfuls Sugar

Make short crust, using 4 oz. flour. Roll out and use to line a shallow baking tin. Mix sugar with coconut, drop in eggs. Mix together with a fork. Spread into the pastry case.

Bake in a moderate oven (Regulo mark 5) for about 30 minutes. When cold, cut with a sharp knife into squares.

PANCAKES

4 oz. Plain Flour
1 level tsp Baking Powder
2 Eggs
Pinch Salt
½ Pint Milk

Sift together flour, baking powder, and salt. Make a well in centre; add beaten eggs and milk gradually, to form a smooth batter, free from lumps.

Melt a small amount of lard in frying pan; when smoking-hot, pour in a thin layer of batter, fry till golden brown, turn and cook on other side.

Lift out, sprinkle with sugar, roll up and serve hot with pieces of lemon or jam or syrup (makes about 8 pancakes).

With self-raising flour, use half the amount of baking powder.

CHERRY CAKES

4 oz. Flour
½ level teaspoonful Baking Powder
2 Eggs
3 oz. Sugar
2 tablespoonfuls Milk
3 oz. Margarine
Angelica
12 Glace Cherries
Icing
Rind of 1 Lemon

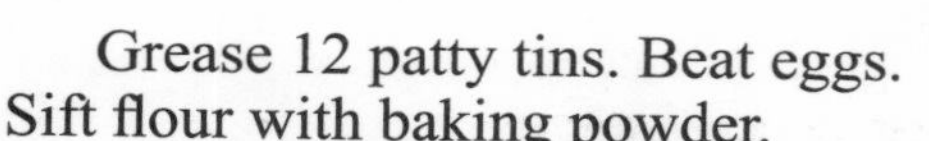

Grease 12 patty tins. Beat eggs. Sift flour with baking powder.

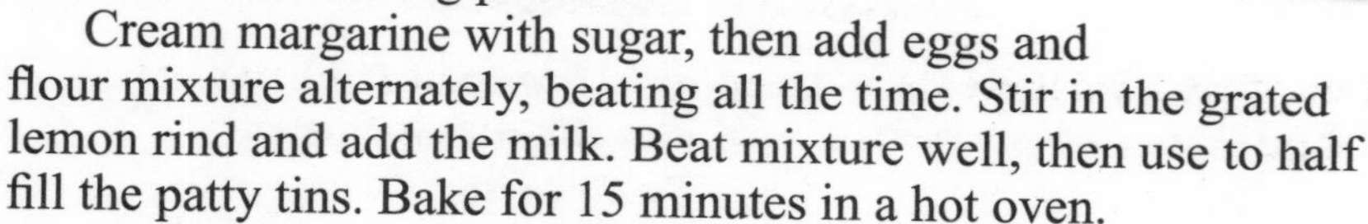

Cream margarine with sugar, then add eggs and flour mixture alternately, beating all the time. Stir in the grated lemon rind and add the milk. Beat mixture well, then use to half fill the patty tins. Bake for 15 minutes in a hot oven.

Cool cakes on a wire tray. Top with white icing when cold, and decorate, arranging two halved cherries on each, with angelica cut to form leaves, and stems piped in green icing.

SCOTCH SHORTBREAD

1 lb. Shortbread Flour
½ lb. Butter or Margarine
4 oz. Castor Sugar

Cream butter and margarine together in a bowl, then gradually sift in small quantities of flour. Knead flour through mixture until the bowl is left clean. Turn on to baking board and continue kneading and adding flour till all flour is used up.

Cut mixture into equal portions and press each piece into shortbread mould, first dusting with a little rice flour or semolina to prevent sticking. Turn out and place on baking sheet, covered with greaseproof paper. Prick top over with a fork.

Place in a moderate oven (Regulo mark 4) and bake until golden brown. These quantities will produce five small cakes of shortbread.

CORN ROUGHS

2 oz. Cornflakes
8 oz. Block Chocolate
1 teaspoonful Sugar

Cut up chocolate and put into a bowl with the sugar. Stand over a pan of hot water, and, without allowing chocolate to get hot, have it melted and soft. Stir in the cornflakes lightly so that they do not break. Using two forks, place mixture in heaps on waxed or greaseproof paper and stand aside until quite set. A few raisins, stoned and halved, may be added with the cornflakes if desired.

ECCLES CAKES

8 oz. Flaky Pastry
2 oz. Caster Sugar
1 oz. Raisins
1 Egg
1 oz. Shredded Peel
Grated Nutmeg
1½ oz. Butter
3 oz. Currants

Melt butter and add the cleaned fruit, finely-shredded peel, and sugar, with a grating of nutmeg. Roll out pastry fairly thin and cut into rounds. Place a spoonful of the fruit mixture on one round, cover with another round, pressing the edges tightly together. Roll with rolling pin until the fruit shows through. Brush with beaten egg and place on a greased baking tin. Bake in a moderate oven (Regulo 4) for 20 minutes. When ready, dust with castor sugar.

PIG'S EARS

Flaky Pastry (as much to make as many as you require)
Castor Sugar

Roll out pastry fairly thin to oblong shape. Turn in the two short ends to meet in the centre. Now fold in two, so that one folded edge lies on top of the other. With a sharp knife cut into thin slices. Dust with castor sugar and space out flat on a greased baking tray. Bake in a hot oven for 10 to 15 minutes.

Cool on a wire tray and, when cold, spread thinly with water icing, if wished.

DUNDEE CAKE

8 oz. Flour
2 Eggs
1 teaspoonful Baking Powder
6 oz. Butter
6 oz. Castor Sugar
A little milk (if necessary)
6 oz. Currants
4 oz. Sultanas
3 oz. Chopped Raisins
2 oz. Chopped Mixed Peel
2 oz. Almonds
Grated rind of ¼ Lemon
¼ teaspoonful Grated Nutmeg
1 teaspoonful Ground Cinnamon

Cream the butter and sugar together in a basin and add eggs, well-beaten, one at a time. Mix in the sieved flour, spice and baking powder, cleaned fruit, one ounce of peeled and chopped almonds, and lemon rind. Add milk if necessary, but the mixture should not be too moist.

Place the cake in prepared tin, sprinkle over the remainder of the almonds, and bake in a moderate oven (Regulo mark 4) for about 2 hours. Cool on wire sieve or rack.

MADEIRA CAKE

½ lb. Flour
5 oz. Butter
3 Eggs
5 oz. Castor Sugar
1 teaspoonful Baking Powder
1 Lemon Rind
Citron peel

Sift flour twice. Cream butter and sugar and stir in the grated rind of lemon. Break eggs separately into a bowl, but do not beat.

Add flour and eggs alternately and by degrees to the mixture, beating well. Finally add baking powder with the last spoonful of flour. Turn into a greased and papered tin.

Cut two thin crescents of citron peel and place on top.

Bake in a moderate oven (Regulo mark 4) for about 1 hour.

Chapter 2

The Icing Age

THIS is one of the most fascinating chapters in this book. The expertise that would be required to ice cakes grows in complexity over the decade.

You can almost track the progress of home bakers becoming ever more skilled, ever more confident and ever more adventurous. You can see the start of the upwards curve that leads to the fantastic cake creations that are celebrated today on television and in the work of bespoke bakers.

The people icing cakes and passing on tips here are the mothers and grandmothers of the great British home baking tradition. It is their skills, swapped and studied in newspaper and magazine pages, that provided the foundations for our modern era in which skilled (and highly opinionated) cake bakers are national superstars.

July 23, 1950.

OIL ICING — When icing a cake, add a teaspoonful of glycerine to the icing sugar when beating it. No cracks will appear when you cut the cake. — **Miss M. Gallacher, The Abbey, North Berwick.**

September 3, 1950.
ICING SUGAR — To prevent icing sugar from going into little hard lumps, roll out with a rolling pin, then add one tablespoonful of cornflour to one pound of sugar. Mix well together and store in an airtight jar. — **Miss A. O. MacInnes, Dunara, Ardrishaig.**

December 3, 1950.
ICED CAKE — If you find you can't return your iced Xmas cake to the tin after icing, place it on the upturned lid and use the tin as the cover. It will be much easier to handle. — **Miss M. Hodgson, 91 Greystone Road, Carlisle.**

December 10, 1950.
ICING — When making white icing for the Xmas cake, add lemon juice. It prevents the icing going hard. — **Mrs E. Muers, 19 Cecil Street, Sunderland.**

December 17, 1950.
SAVES SUGAR — Here is an easily made icing using no sugar. Mix the required quantity of sweetened condensed milk and desiccated coconut to a stiff paste. Spread thickly over the cake, using a wetted knife. Then press the cake, icing downwards, into a plate of loose coconut. Shake off surplus coconut. — **Mrs C. A. Ballardie, 67 Kintore Road, Newlands, Glasgow.**

August 19, 1951.
ICING — If you do not have an icing set, drop the pourer top of a salt pot into a cone of greaseproof paper. Cut the end so that the pourer just shows through the paper. This will do simple lettering and decoration. — **Mrs N. Wilson, 85 Bankhead Avenue, Bucksburn, Aberdeenshire.**

April 5, 1953.
ICING SUGAR — If your icing sugar has formed a solid lump, rub it on the carrot grater to reduce it to powder again. — **Mrs M. Dixon, Kingfield, Annerley Road, Annan.**

July 26, 1953
NEW ICING — If short of icing sugar, cream a cup of brown sugar, 1 tablespoonful butter and 1 tablespoonful boiling water. Add few drops lemon juice. — **Mrs R. Kerr, 34 West High Street, Forfar.**

December26, 1954.
ICING — When using royal icing, keep a damp cloth over the bowl. This keeps the icing from forming a skin before the cake decorating is finished. — **Mrs M. Carmichael, 28 Wylie Avenue, Alexandria.**

May 8, 1955.
ICING TEA CAKES — A simple way of icing cakes is to dip them into the icing rather than spread it on each cake. It's much quicker. — **Mrs Price, 17 Victoria Road, Yeovil.**

August 28, 1955.
ICING — When colouring icing, use an eye dropper. It helps to get just the right shade. — **Mrs P. Martin, 120d Graham Street, Airdrie.**

November 18, 1956.
ICING FOR CAKE — When covering the top of my Christmas cake with almond icing, I roll out the icing, place the tin the cake was baked in on the icing, and cut round it. The icing then fits the cake perfectly. — **Mrs E. Dainty, 48 Honor Avenue, Goldthorn Park, Wolverhampton.**

February 10, 1957.
UNUSUAL ICING — Bring four tablespoons of red jam slowly to the boil, and boil for a minute. Pour it over a stiffly beaten egg white, and beat until mixture is stiff. Pour at once over a plain cake for a tasty and unusual icing. — **Mrs M. Thompson, 12 Davidson Street, Lancaster.**

August 25, 1957.
ICING — When icing a cake with a syringe, the mixture often becomes thick and difficult to squeeze out. Hold syringe under the hot water tap and the icing flows freely. — **Mrs M. Dow, 162 High Street, Laurencekirk.**

December 15, 1957.
ICING BAG — The silver foil wrapping on margarine, complete with its paper lining, makes a perfect icing bag. Twist it in into a cone and snip off a tiny piece at the point. — **Miss J. Fowlie, Ardgowan, Strathpeffer, wins a pair of towels.**

May 4, 1958.
QUICK ICING — To ice a cake quickly, grate chocolate over it as soon as it is removed from the oven. Return to oven for a moment or two until the chocolate melts. — **Mrs C. Preston, 85 Brockburn Road, Glasgow, wins a pair of towels.**

August 24, 1958.
CAKE CUTTING — When cutting a round iced cake into even slices, stretch a thread across the icing and press lightly down. This prevents the icing cracking. — **Mrs C. Brown, 480 Tollcross Road, Glasgow.**

November 2, 1958.
WHEN ICING — Many kitchen stools are adjustable. Try using one as an icing turntable when icing a birthday or Christmas cake. The job is much easier done. — **Mrs McLaughlin, 8 Thomson Road, Rosyth.**

November 9, 1958.
QUICK ICING — Place chocolate peppermint creams on cake immediately after removing from oven. As patties melt, spread chocolate over cake in marble effect. — **Mrs A. Yeaman, 4 Featherhall Grove, Edinburgh.**

January 25, 1959.
FLAVOURED ICING — When you want to give icing a little colour and flavour, melt one half-teaspoonful of raspberry jelly crystals in a little water and add to the icing. — **A. McMurray, 44 Shuna Street, Glasgow.**

February 22, 1959.
ICING — When making icing for a cake, add a teaspoonful of condensed milk to the mixture. Then it doesn't crack or fall off the cake. — **Mrs C. B. Ross, 80 Beaufort Gardens, Bishopbriggs.**

June 21, 1959.
SAVES TIME — To save time and patience when putting meringue mixture into icing bag, clip one side of the bag to the mixing bowl with a small-size plastic clothes peg. — **Mrs Barbara M. Arnott, 22 Eskdale Street, Glasgow.**

August 16, 1959.
SIMPLE ICING — A simple way to ice buns is to pop a piece of cooking chocolate on each one as soon as they are taken out of the oven and spread with a knife dipped in hot water. — **Mrs Margaret Craig, 37 Kilburn Street, Donegal Road, Belfast.**

September 27, 1959.
CAKES — I find it a great help when icing cakes (particularly for children) to add a cube of table jelly to the water icing. This not only provides colouring but flavouring as well. — **Mrs E. Ramsden, Acairseid, New Romney.**

December 6, 1959.
ICING — If the royal icing on your Christmas cake doesn't harden owing to the damp atmosphere, place the cake carefully in a warm (not hot) oven after the gas has been turned out. Close the door and leave for an hour or so. — **Mrs D. Tucker, 84 The Avenue, Wilton, Salisbury.**

December 20, 1959.
NOVELTY ICING — Ice the children's cake with white icing on top and pink round the side. Decorate top with conversation sweets placed so that each child receives one with a piece of cake. — **M. Wilson c/o Beech Cliffe, 409 Warbreck Drive, Bispham, Blackpool.**

December 20, 1959.
BETTER ICING — When plain white icing is required, replace one tablespoonful of icing sugar with the same amount of cornflour. This keeps the icing thick, makes it softer to cut, and prevents cracking. **— Mrs D. Bruce, 36 Kinloch Street, Carnoustie.**

The Icing Makes Them Dainty

When making little iced cakes first prepare some round or fancy-shaped tins. Grease them and dust with a mixture of flour and sugar.

After creaming the butter, grate a little lemon rind and add it to the creamed butter. Then mix in sugar and salt thoroughly.

Sieve the flour and add half of it with one egg. Mix and beat, then add the remainder of the flour and the other egg. Beat again.

Sprinkle in the baking powder, then half fill the prepared tins with the mixture. Bake in a moderate oven.

When the cakes are ready turn them out of the moulds on to a wire sieve to cool. Then spread on a layer of thick icing.

Decorate the tops with crystallised cherries or violets. Any little sponge cakes can be finished in this way. For a suitable recipe see Queen Cakes on page 40.

Chapter 3

Jams And Jars

THE jammy (or jeely) piece could make a fairly strong claim to be regarded as Scotland's national children's dish. We all remember the delicious joys of jammy sandwiches.

And you will have, in your mind's eye, a picture of your mother or grandmother making jam in that big pot she had, or pickling the many things that were pickled in those days.

The jam-makers and picklers of our childhoods deserve to be remembered and celebrated. And it doesn't matter whether you were a fan of the strawberry, raspberry or bramble kind of jam — they were all good.

As you read these tips you may find a strange feeling growing in your stomach. That feeling is a longing for a jeely piece. When did you last have a jeely piece?

July 30, 1950.
JAM — When making jam, add a teaspoonful of glycerine to each lb. It brings out the flavour of the fruit and prevents moulding. — **Mrs John Wallace, 45 Market Street, Brechin.**

July 30, 1950.
PICKLES — Put a teaspoonful of mustard into a small muslin bag and pop into the jar containing pickled beetroot. It keeps the pickle fresh longer. — **Mrs Whitelaw, 69 Carrick Drive, Glasgow.**

March 12, 1950.
QUICK MARMALADE — To peel oranges and lemons quickly for marmalade, soak them for a few minutes in boiling water, and the pith will come away with the rind. — **Nancy Kennedy, Aden Hotel, Old Deer, Mintlaw, Aberdeenshire.**

August 12, 1951.
GOOSEBERRIES — To keep gooseberries whole while stewing, boil the water and sugar together first. Put the berries in while the syrup is still boiling. They will be done in a few minutes. — **Mrs M. Finlay, Sea View, Innellan, Argyllshire.**

August 19, 1951.
SEEDLESS — Wash 4 lb. gooseberries and cover with water. Bring to boil until soft. Rub through a sieve until there are just the seeds left. These should be thrown away. Leave to stand overnight. Now measure bowl of juice for bowl of sugar and boil for 15 minutes until it jellies in saucer. Don't forget the lump of butter to prevent scum. — **Mrs D. Scott, 27 Summer Road, Wemyss, Fife.**

June 24, 1951.
JAM MAKING — A few drops of salad oil rubbed well over the bottom of the preserving pan before using will prevent the jam from sticking to the bottom. — **Mrs D. Lamond, Edinburgh.**

July 15, 1951.
THICKENS JAM — If jam will not jell, sprinkle a little seed tapioca or sago into it and boil up again for a little while. The tapioca or sago will be quite invisible and the jam quite firm. I allow 1 teaspoonful to every pound of jam. — **Mrs V. M. Cormack, 66 Eastwoodmains Road, Giffnock, Glasgow.**

July 15, 1951.
JAM TIP — Strawberry jam made this way retains its full fruit flavour after keeping a whole year. Cover 6 lb. strawberries with 5 lb. sugar and leave overnight. Put in the preserving pan with two teaspoonfuls tartaric acid and bring to boil. After ten minutes fast boiling, set the pan in cold water and keep stirring the jam till slightly cool, then pot. — **Mrs D. Brown, Mill Farm, Carnock, Dunfermline.**

July 6, 1952.
SAVES BERRIES — I hope to enjoy my strawberries this summer. In the beds I've put several small bottles filled with household ammonia, loosely tamped with cotton wool. The wool attracts the birds, but one whiff and they never come back. I think even slugs keep away. — **Miss M. Brown, 17 Ulster Drive, Edinburgh.**

July 20, 1952.
JAMPOT COVERS — Mix a dessertspoonful cornflour with cold water, add boiling water till thick. Cut up discs of paper from clean bags, dip both sides in cornflour, place on top of jam jars while jam is still boiling hot. This makes firm jampot covers which will keep for years. — **Mrs Tungall, 21 Muirpark, Eskbank, Midlothian.**

August 10, 1952.
PLUM JAM — In preparing plums for jam, make an incision at the stalk end of each plum. The stones will pop out and rise to the surface. — **Miss A. Urquhart, Culliecudden, by Conon, Ross-shire.**

September 21, 1952.
CANDIED PEEL — Pare rind from oranges and lemons, chop finely and store in screwtop jar with a little honey. The honey soon candies. Add a teaspoonful or more to any cake mixture to give it an excellent flavour. — **Mrs Walsh, 130 Barlow Street, Preston.**

April 6, 1952.
MUSTARD — If freshly-made mustard is put straight into a screw-top jar, it'll always be ready for use and will keep fresh till the jar is empty. — **Margaret O. Bell, 18 Westlands, Sunderland.**

June 22, 1952.
JAM MAKING — Before starting, rub preserving pan with olive oil. Jam won't burn even when boiled quickly. — **N. Kennedy, 4 Burn Road, Inverness.**

January 20, 1952.
MARMALADE TIPS — Put half a teaspoonful baking soda in the preserving pan when marmalade is boiling. It will soften the skins. To spread shreds equally throughout, leave the marmalade in the pan for 15 minutes after taking off heat — **Mrs M. Martin, 6 Kinloss Crescent, Cupar.**

February 10, 1952.
MARMALADE — If a carrot is grated and added to marmalade oranges while soaking, the preserve will have a beautiful rich colour. — **Mrs J. Clark, Victoria Terrace, Airdrie.**

August 9, 1953.
The Very Thing For Filling Jam Jars — The metal neck of a vacuum flask is handy for filling jam pots. Unscrew and place it upside down on the jars. It prevents loss of jam — and scalded hands. After use, it's easily replaced on the flask again. — **Mrs Winton, 12 Back Lebanon, Cupar, wins a pair of towels.**

July 19, 1953.
JAM PRESERVER — When jam is set, brush over with pastry brush dipped in vinegar. The jam will keep for an indefinite period and will not mildew. — **Mrs Jenny Ross, 28 Craigpark Drive, Glasgow.**

August 9, 1953.
MUSTARD — When preparing mustard, add a pinch of salt to prevent discoloration, and a little olive oil to prevent it drying hard. — **Miss I. I. Langlands, 55 Forfar Road, Dundee.**

August 30, 1953.
STORING JAM — Jam should be kept somewhere warm and dry, and on no account near anything damp (dampness combined with warmth accelerates mould). An ideal place is a cupboard in the kitchen with a small grill at side to let in fresh air. — **Mrs R. Robertson, Glasgow.**

June 27, 1954.
EASY-MADE CHUTNEY — Keep the vinegar left over from pickled onions and fill up the jar with stoned and chopped dates. Leave for a week, then stir well, and you've a delicious, sweet chutney. — **Mrs R. Davidson, 16 Woodlands Crescent, Turriff.**

October 3, 1954.
APPLES — When preparing apples for bottling, peel them into a basin of salted water. This preserves their whiteness. — **C. F. Jardine, Edinburgh.**

January 23, 1955.
MARMALADE — When preparing fruit for marmalade I use a potato peeler to cut off rind, then shred with a knife. This makes a very fine shred. — **Mrs E. H. Henry, Causewayhead, Carlisle.**

May 1, 1955.
JAMS — Fill jars to the very top when making jams and jellies. The wax tissues fit snugly, keep all air out, and are easily removed. — **Mrs G. Wallace, 21 Glenbervie Rd., Aberdeen.**

June 5, 1955.
SECRET OF MAKING STRAWBERRY JAM — When making strawberry jam, don't pot it until the jam is cool, otherwise the berries rise to the top. — **Mrs Clifford, 45 Old Mill Road, Southwick, Sunderland, wins a pair of towels.**

June 26, 1955.
JAM COVERS — If transparent jam pot covers are difficult to come apart, lay them in the sun for a few minutes, and they separate easily. — **Miss L. Greig, Dunearn, Fetterangus.**

August 21, 1955.
GIFT — When making jam, pour the small amounts left over into paste jars and seal. A box of four makes an acceptable gift for an invalid or friend living alone. — **Mrs C. Gray, Star, Markinch.**

September 11, 1955.
JAM-MAKING — A child's small, wooden beach spade is excellent for stirring jam. It's longer than the ordinary wooden spoon, and doesn't slip into the pan. — **Mrs Salisbury, 6 Primrose Terrace, Mill Hill, Blackburn, Lancs.**

September 11, 1955.
FRUIT SCONES — When making damson jam, a quick and easy way to remove the stones which come to the top when boiling is to use old sugar tongs. — **Mrs M. Cameron, The Neuk, Muirhall Road, Perth.**

September 25, 1955.
DAMSON JAM — I use a long-handled, perforated spoon to remove stones when the jam is boiling. I find it easy. — **Mrs R. Brown, Sornhill Cottages, Galston.**

October 30, 1955.
PARSLEY STORAGE — To preserve parsley for winter use, store in airtight jars. Use salt and parsley in alternate layers, one-inch deep when pressed down firmly. — **Mrs A. Hearton, 1 Bradan Avenue, Bellsbank, Dalmellington.**

July 22, 1956.
A TIP FOR STORING JAM — The labelling of jam takes a long time. Where shelves are set apart for storing, a good plan is to put a strip of wood between each kind of jam and tack a card with name and date on front of shelf. — **Mrs Cuthbert, 20 Vine Park Avenue, Kilmaurs, Kilmarnock, wins a pair of towels.**

August 5, 1956.
FILLING JAM JARS — Use a gravy boat to transfer the jam from pan to jar. The boat is easily dipped in the jam, and the narrow, long mouth fits into jars of any size. — **Mrs McCormick, 136 Levern Crescent, Barrhead.**

August 5, 1956.
JAM MAKING — Screw a small hook into the end of the stick, spurtle, or wooden spoon you use to stir your jam. Then, when you are not stirring, hook the spurtle over the side of the pan. This prevents it slipping into the jam. — **D. Robertson, 10 Cummingair Drive, Motherwell.**

August 19, 1956.
JAM COVERING — When covering jam, instead of moistening the clear covers which are inclined to curl, moisten round rim and neck of jar then fix covers on. The job is done in half the time. — **Mrs Agnes Mitchell, 1 Lint Riggs, Falkirk.**

August 26, 1956.
JAM MAKING — I find it very helpful when filling jam pots to put a rubber glove on the hand holding the jars. It saves being burnt with hot splashes. — **Mrs T. Riddell, 187 Gala Park Road, Galashiels.**

September 2, 1956.
PICKLES — Sugar tongs are excellent for serving pickles, and save the bother of chasing them round the jar. — **Miss Elizabeth Taylor, 24 Leven Street, Glasgow.**

September 30, 1956.
FRUIT BOTTLING — When preparing pears for bottling, use a teaspoon for scooping out the centres. — **Mrs Catherine Thomson, 100 Hardy Street, Hull.**

February 17, 1957.
JAM COVERING — It takes only seconds to cover jam pots with gummed covers if these are moistened over a steaming kettle. This avoids messy handling and ensures good sealing. — **Mrs Jean Pert, 20 McGregor Avenue, Airdrie.**

May 26, 1957.
FOR JAM TIME — Buy an extra 2 lb. of sugar each week for laying aside for jam-making time. Then the expense isn't so heavy all at one time. — **Mrs F. Moore, 10 Torogay Street, Glasgow.**

June 30, 1957.
GOOSEBERRY JAM — When making gooseberry jam add a few cloves. The jam has a lovely flavour. — **Mrs McColm, Whiteleys, Stranraer.**

July 14, 1957.
MILDEW ON JAM — To prevent jam from getting mildew, dip rounds of greaseproof paper in the white of an egg. Place on top of the jam and seal in the usual way. — **Mrs Betty Owen, Arvonia, Dolwyddelen, wins a pair of towels.**

July 14, 1957.
JAM MAKING — When filling jam jars, use a sauce boat. It saves time and there are no sticky jars to wash afterwards. — **Mrs R. Walker, 16 Burns Street, Irvine.**

August 11, 1957.
RHUBARB JAM — When using preserved ginger in making rhubarb jam, grate the ginger instead of cutting it. The ginger is more evenly distributed through the jam, and makes it easier to spread. — **A. Johnstone, Burn Row, Slamannan.**

August 25, 1957.
BANANA MARMALADE — Take 10 firm bananas, 1 lb. sugar, and juice of three lemons. Slice bananas finely. Place all ingredients in pan and boil gently for about half an hour or until the mixture is the consistency of jam. Stir constantly to avoid burning. This makes a good filling for cakes or sandwiches. — **Mrs A. Livingstone, Druan, Helensburgh.**

October 13, 1957.
JAM — Don't put home-made jam on the top shelf of the cupboard. Hot air rises. Store on the bottom shelf and you will have good results. — **E. Harris, Post Office Stores, Hatfield Heath, Herts.**

January 26, 1958.
MARMALADE-MAKING — Before putting marmalade into hot jars leave it in the pan 15 minutes or so. Then the shreds of peel are evenly distributed, and don't sink to the bottom. — **Mrs Slater, 17 Geddes Avenue, Portknockie, wins a pair of towels.**

May 4, 1958.
APRICOT JAM — Put the dried fruit through the mincer before soaking. It softens quicker, and the jam has a much nicer consistency. — **Mrs M. Mackinnon, 14 Percy Street, Ibrox, Glasgow.**

July 6, 1958.
USE THE MINCER — Put gooseberries through the mincer when making jam. The work is quicker, the jam sets more firmly, and there are no coarse skins in the jam. — **C. D. McKinimie, Huntly.**

July 6, 1958.
RHUBARB JAM — When soaking rhubarb for jam, put rhubarb and sugar time about in dish, starting with rhubarb and finishing with sugar. By doing so the sugar melts quickly. — **Mrs Jon Morrison, Crudie Croft, Turriff.**

August 17, 1958.
NO CURLING — When covering jam with transparent discs, damp the neck of the jar and apply the disc dry. This gives a neat and effective result and prevents the disc from curling. — **Mrs Dorothy Allan, Rhuallan Trian, Cawdor Road, Nairn, wins a pair of towels.**

August 24, 1958.
JAM-MAKING — When making jam with stoned fruit, hang a small wire soap basket inside the jam pan, skim off stones as they rise and place in basket to drain. — **Mrs M. Wright, 71 Clydesdale Avenue, Paisley.**

September 14, 1958.
DAMSON JAM — When making damson jam, boil fruit till tender, then put through a colander. Add 1 lb. sugar to each pound of pulp. This makes a delicious jam without the small stones. — **Mrs B. Mitchell, 9 Viewforth, Edinburgh.**

September 21, 1958.
APPLE JELLY — When making apple jelly, add a handful of rowans. This gives the jelly a nice colour and piquant flavour. — **Mrs S. A. Grant, 51a Duke Street, Huntly.**

January 18, 1959.
MARMALADE MAKING — When making marmalade, use the centre section of a coffee percolator instead of muslin bag for boiling the pips. It does the job much better as the juice of the marmalade is constantly passing through, taking with it the pectin which helps the marmalade to set. — **Mrs J. Brown, 64 Grange Estate, Church Crookham, Nr. Aldershot.**

February 1, 1959.
FOR A CHANGE — Instead of flavouring rhubarb jam with ginger, try mixed spice. Lovely taste! — **Sister H. Pollock, St Ann's General Hospital, London.**

April 26, 1959.
JAM COVERING — Moisten the covers with vinegar instead of water to help prevent moulding of jam. — **Miss H. Scott, Newstead, Melrose.**

May 17, 1959.
JAM MAKING — When making jam this year, fill each jar to the top as there is always shrinkage throughout the months of storage. **— Margaret Henderson, 6 Ardbeg Street, Glasgow.**

May 31, 1959.
JAM POT COVERS — When transparent jam pot covers have stuck together, place them on a warmed plate and press with the hand. In a few seconds the edges curl and the covers are easily separated. — **Mrs M. Baxter, 53 Birkenside, Gorebridge.**

June 28, 1959.
RHUBARB JAM — A delightful and inexpensive way to flavour rhubarb jam with ginger is to add a 1 lb. jar of ginger marmalade to the jam when almost ready. — **Mrs Dixon, Mhorile, Grantown-on-Spey.**

July 12, 1959.
FOR JAM POTTING — When pouring hot jam into warmed jars, it's helpful to stand the jars in a wire chip basket. Hold this in the left hand near saucepan and ladle jam with right. This saves hot jam spilling over your fingers. — **Mrs A. Stow, 28 Murray Rd., Rugby.**

July 19, 1959.
SAVE THE FRUIT — When gathering berries from bushes, spread clean sacking or brown paper under each bush. This keeps clean any berries which fall. It's surprising the amount of fruit that can be salvaged in this way. — **Tom Macaulay, Sen., 33 Wynd, Cumbernauld, Glasgow.**

August 30, 1959.
JAM COVERS — I have found it a great saving when making a lot of jam to buy a roll of Cellophane and packet of rubber bands. I make my own covers by shaping with a saucer to fit round top of jars. — **Mrs S. A. Grant, 51a Duke Street, Huntly.**

September 20, 1959.
JELLY — When boiling berries to strain for jelly, use the potato masher instead of the jelly spoon. In this way you can crush the pulp while the fruit is boiling, thus extracting the maximum amount of juice. — **Mrs M. Smith, 59 Moor Lane, Netherton, Huddersfield.**

September 20, 1959.
CHUTNEY — When making tomato chutney, skin the tomatoes last. You then find all stains gone from your fingers after doing the apples and onions. — **Mrs Berry, 13 Craigs Gardens, Edinburgh.**

October 18, 1959.
PICKLES — When making pickles, rinse out the jars with cold vinegar before bottling to prevent fermentation. — **Mrs M. Thompson, 12 Davidson Street, Lancaster.**

Cookery Nook

BATTER FOR FISH.—When mixing batter, add a tablespoonful of vinegar to the mixture. The batter will stick more closely to the fish. There is no taste of vinegar.

BISCUITS.—Keep fresh by putting in a Polythene bag before putting them away in a tin.
A few cubes of sugar in the bottom of the tin will also help.

BUTTER.—When measuring for baking, cut butter and fat diagonally from corner to corner. This gives a more accurate measure.

CAKE MIXING.—When creaming cake mixtures you'll find it easier if you place a damp cloth under the bowl. This prevents bowl sliding about.

CAKE MIXTURE.—To prevent cake mixture sticking to the wooden spoon it's a good idea to first rub the spoon well with greased paper.
Before putting cake mixture into cases, dip the spoon in hot water and the mixture will drop off easily.

CAKE TINS.—Before storing cakes, line tin with blotting paper to absorb moisture. This will keep the food fresh and the tins rust-free.

CHOPS AND STEAK.—When frying, insert the fork in the fat to turn instead of in the meat. This will prevent the juices from running.

COOKERY BOOK.—Keep clean while cooking by slipping a Polythene bag over the page you are using. This will also keep the book open at the right place.

EGGS.—Before breaking eggs for poaching or frying, put them in boiling water for half a minute to prevent the white from spreading in the pan.
A cracked egg can still be boiled by rubbing over the crack with dripping before putting the egg in water.

FANCY CAKES.—To store, place a teacup in the middle of the tin, place the cakes round it, rest a plate on top of the cup and fill the second layer with more cakes.

FLANS.—Before making a flan cut two strips of greaseproof paper and lay them across the tin in the shape of a cross. Leave the ends projecting above the top. When cooked, the flan can be lifted out by the paper strips without breaking.

FISH.—To keep fresh in warm weather, lay on a plate, cover with greaseproof paper and sprinkle the paper with cooking salt.

FRIED FISH.—To prevent fish sticking to the pan, sprinkle a little salt in the pan before putting in the fat.

FROSTING.—Dip the rims of the glasses to be frosted for party drinks in lemon juice, then in sugar and leave to set.

GLASS JARS.—To prevent from cracking when hot jam or jelly is poured in, stand a wooden fork or spoon in the jar.

HARD-BOILED EGGS.—Put in cold water for a few minutes, then tap the shell all over with a knife. The shell will then come off all in one piece.

HOT DISHES.—To remove hot dishes from the oven, place them on a meat tin or baking sheet to provide a better hold.

JAM-MAKING.—Screw a cup hook into the top of the wooden spoon you are using. It can then be hung on the edge of the pan between stirrings.
Scum can be prevented by dropping a piece of butter into the pan when it is boiling. Never skim jam too soon as it is only froth which rises at first.

JAM POT COVERS.—If these become glued together, lay a thin paper over them and press with a warm iron.

Left—Cut a large fruit cake in the middle and take slices from the centre, then push halves together again to keep moist and in good condition.

Above—Place two strips of greaseproof paper crosswise in the tin before baking a flan. When ready, the flan can be lifted out easily by the projecting ends of the paper.

6

Chapter 4

Perfect Puddings

THERE are many of us, probably too many of us, who would declare for some sort of pudding, dessert or sweetmeat as their favourite dish from childhood. Scotland isn't known for its skinnymalinky waistlines.

So spare a thought for the mother and housewife who had to concoct perfect puddings when sugar rationing didn't finally end until September 1953.

Personally, my favourite was a rice pudding. I loved it, and still do. Nothing brings back memories of childhood to me more than a baked rice pudding, with a brown skin on top and ruinously sweet, stodgy rice below.

My father used to call it "ambrosia, food of the gods".

He was right.

September 10, 1950.

SUGAR SAVER — Here's a rich and economical milk pudding. Put a pint of water into a saucepan and bring to the boil. Put in two or three tablespoonfuls sweetened condensed milk, a nub of butter or margarine, and a pinch of salt, then add whatever padding is desired. — **Mrs J. L. Henderson, North Lodge, Western Avenue, Perth.**

F-r-u-i-t-i-e-r Jelly

It's JELL-O !

FLAVOUR-SEALED—till the moment you make it! The moment Jell-O crystals dissolve you'll realise this is a different jelly. Fruitier! That's because Jell-O's fresh-fruit flavour is actually sealed into each crystal by an exclusive process. When the crystal dissolves the flavour escapes. Not before! So Jell-O saves *all* its flavour for you!

FRUITIER—the moment you taste it!

How much fruitier Jell-O tastes! The flavour-saving secret of Jell-O crystals keeps that flavour fresh as the fruit itself. Pop a sparkling spoonful into your mouth and . . . M-m-m! FRUITIER! That's Jell-O joy! And yet the price is only 8d. a packet, so why not get one or two next time you're shopping?

7 fruitier flavours: Strawberry, Raspberry, Orange, Lemon, Lime, Blackcurrant and exclusive Orchard Delight.

MADE BY BIRD'S

8d. each

November 12, 1950.
DUMPLING — When making a "clootie" dumpling, after scalding and flouring the cloth, drape inside bowl or colander, then pour in mixture. This keeps the mixture from spreading over the cloth too far before ends are gathered up for tying. — **Mrs C. W. Calder, 1533 Dumbarton Road, Glasgow.**

February 11, 1951.
LUMPY PUDDINGS — If your milk pudding has turned out lumpy, beating with the egg switch will smooth out all the lumps beautifully. — **Mrs H. Hood, 22 Pennycook Lane, Dundee.**

April 8, 1951.
EGGLESS — Mix 1 lb. of self-raising flour, two dessertspoonfuls condensed milk, and a dessertspoonful sugar to a smooth paste with water. Bake on girdle. When about to serve, drop the pancakes into a saucepan containing smoking hot fat for about two minutes, or until they turn a golden brown. They're a treat for tea. — **Mrs C. McEwan, 25 Inglish Street, Dennistoun, Glasgow.**

May 13, 1951.
PANCAKES — A dessertspoonful olive oil added to pancake batter keeps pancakes deliciously soft for a few days. — **Miss S. McArthur, 2 Balornock Rd., Glasgow.**

May 13, 1951.
SAGO FOR SUET — When making a steamed pudding, steep four tablespoonfuls sago overnight and use instead of suet. Your puddings will be lighter. — **Mrs B. Finnie, Bridge Street, Ballater.**

May 27, 1951.
GRAPEFRUIT — No sugar is required when grapefruit is served in this way. Peel grapefruit and cut up. Put in a small saucepan with very little water. Add two or three tablespoonfuls syrup. Bring very gently to the boil, and simmer slowly until tender. Serve cold. — **J. Mack, 131 Pumpherston Road, Broxburn.**

June 3, 1951.
MILK PUDDINGS — If some sugar is sprinkled on top of a custard or other milk pudding before it begins to cool, no skin will form on top. — **Mrs H. Allan, 7 Fish Street, Aberdeen.**

July 1, 1951.
CARAMEL SAUCE — Before lining a bowl with suet paste for a fruit pudding, lard it well and sprinkle some Demerara sugar round the sides and the bottom. When the pudding is turned out, the sugar forms a brown caramel sauce. — **Miss E. Bremner, 131 Comiston Road, Edinburgh.**

October 7, 1951.
APPLES — Stew about 1 lb. apples in a little water and sweeten slightly. Melt an orange jelly in ¾ pint of boiling water and add to apples. Leave overnight. The apples take on a lovely orange flavour and are set in the jelly. — **Mrs H. T. Robb, Holestane, Thornhill, Dumfries-shire.**

December 16, 1951.
SOFT FRUITS — Cherries and dates for cakes and puddings can be chopped easily if they are first rolled in plain flour. The pieces don't stick together, and fewer cherries and dates are needed. — **Miss Wilson, F. L. F. Ground, Fulwell Road, Sunderland.**

December 16, 1951.
PASTRY GLAZE — To glaze pastry without using eggs, boil together one tablespoonful brown sugar with two tablespoonfuls milk till dissolved. When cool, brush over pastry. It makes a lovely brown crust. — **Mrs Isabella Clark, 2 McLeod Crescent, Prestonpans.**

January 6, 1952.
CUSTARD — To make successful baked custard, always boil the milk first, allow to cool, then add the beaten egg and sugar. — **Margaret O. Bell, 18 Westlands, Sunderland.**

TAKE BROWN & POLSON
FLAVOURED CORNFLOUR
AND MAKE
Stuffed Pineapple Blancmange
Make a blancmange with the contents of the Pineapple envelope in the 5-flavour packet of Brown & Polson Flavoured Cornflour. (You'll find full instructions on the packet.) Wet a tumbler, place it in the centre of a wetted mould or basin and pour the blancmange around it. When set, remove the tumbler and turn out the blancmange. Fill the centre with fruit, and, if desired, top with cream. Equally delicious made with Raspberry, Strawberry, Caramel or Banana Flavoured Cornflour.
Brown & Polson
table talk
THIS FRUIT PUDDING IS QUICKEST OF ALL
FINISH YOUR CAKE WITH
Spicy Crunch
SOMETHING SIMPLE FOR SUPPER
It's made for enjoyment when it's made with
Brown & Polson

April 20, 1952.
DUMPLING — Lift your "clootie" dumpling on to a colander or sieve instead of a plate. The water drips away and so keeps the dumpling drier and easier to handle. **— Mrs J. Watt, Edenbank, Strathmiglo.**

July 13, 1952.
CUSTARDS — Baked custards will not be watery if a few grains of rice are put into the bottom of the dish. The rice absorbs any moisture and leaves the custard firm. Breadcrumbs can be used instead of rice. **— Mrs M. McCallum, McCallum Street, Campbeltown.**

October 12, 1952.
WON'T BURN — When baking a milk pudding in the oven, place the casserole with pudding inside a pie dish of cold water. The pudding won't burn this way. — **Mrs P. Corkindale, 33 Moulin Circus, Cardonald, Glasgow.**

October 12, 1952.
SUBSTITUTE — Gather bunches of elderberries (they're plentiful just now) and hang them up to dry, either on a clothes pulley or in a very slow oven on an open shelf. They can be used for cakes or puddings. — **Mrs R. MacKinnon, 225 Newlands Road, Cathcart, Glasgow.**

August 16,1953.
NO SKIN CUSTARD — To prevent skin forming on top of custard put in half the amount of sugar. After pouring into dish sprinkle other half over the top. When cold whip up with egg switch. — **Mrs M. Macdonald, 38 Royston Mains Crescent, Edinburgh.**

June 13, 1954.
LUMP-FREE PUDDINGS — When making milk pudding like semolina, sage, tapioca, &c., I use the egg whisk, instead of a wooden spoon, for stirring. It separates the grains easily, and I never have a lumpy pudding. — **Mrs L. Waugh, 18 Wardlaw Street, Edinburgh.**

August 21, 1955.
GOOD FLAVOUR — When making custard pudding, try moist brown sugar instead of usual castor or granulated. Use same amount. It gives a nice caramel flavour. — **Mrs G. B. Allan, 71 Witham Road, Anerley, London.**

August 28, 1955.
CLOOTIE DUMPLING — After having boiled an old-fashioned dumpling, remove cloth and sprinkle sugar immediately over the dumpling. This keeps hard skin from forming. — **Mrs M. Miller, 18 Fordyce Street, Glasgow.**

January 15, 1956.
CUSTARD — When making custard, instead of stirring with a spoon, whip with an egg whisk. It comes up like cream. — **Mrs J. McLaren, Moness, Hanick Terrace, Forfar.**

January 29, 1956.
NICE FLAVOUR — When making milk puddings, stir in a heaped teaspoonful of honey. It gives a nice flavour, and is also very nourishing. — **Mrs I. Riddell, 5 Ardley Terrace, Stonehaven.**

March 11, 1956.
NICE AND LIGHT — When making a steam pudding I use crumbled-down stale sponge cake instead of the usual breadcrumbs. It makes a delicious light and spongy pudding. — **Mrs Gibbon, Cragganholm, Cragganmore, Ballindalloch.**

May 13, 1956.
CUSTARD — To prevent a thick skin forming on pouring custard, stir in a little cold milk after it is made. Put the lid on and leave till ready for use. — **K. Hutchison, 26 Millbrae Terrace, Thankerton, Biggar.**

June 3, 1956.
CURDS — Many children dislike the sour taste of curds. When the milk is warm, add one teaspoonful of sugar to it and pour over the rennet. When set, sprinkle the top with brown sugar or powdered chocolate. — **A. B. Cordiner, Roseacre, Rothes.**

July 29, 1956.
SAUCES — Stir sauces and custards with a perforated spoon. There's less sticking, and the results are smoother. — **Mrs M. B. Brown, 1039 Tollcross Road, Tollcross, Glasgow.**

August 5, 1956.
JELLY — To set a jelly quickly in hot weather, add a teaspoonful of lemon juice to a pint of jelly. The mould containing the jelly should then be set in a flower pot and packed round with kitchen salt. — **Miss A. Watson, 17 Balmeg Avenue, Giffnock.**

September 16, 1956.
STEAMED PUDDING — Knit or crochet a string bag, and put basin with the pudding in the bag. It is easily lifted out when ready without burning fingers. — **Mrs Donaldson, 109 Randolph Drive, Clarkston, Glasgow.**

September 30, 1956.
QUICK SWEET — Reheat a few doughnuts (unringed preferred) in warm oven for two minutes, and roll in brown sugar. Split quickly and spread with hot plum jam, and serve with vanilla custard. — **D. Barty, Dunalistair, Broughty Ferry, Dundee.**

November 18, 1956.
PLUM PUDDINGS — If you are adding rum, brandy, or sherry to your plum pudding, add it to your fruit after having cleaned and picked it over. Leave the fruit in the spirit for 24 hours, stirring occasionally, before adding to the dry ingredients. In this way the spirit is evenly distributed, with the full flavour through the mixture. — **Mrs Skilling, 79 Alexandra Parade, Glasgow.**

February 3, 1957.
YORKSHIRE PUDDING — Dispense with the trouble of working egg into flour when making batter for Yorkshire pudding. Whisk the egg with the milk, and sieve in the flour. Twice as easy and just as successful. — **Mrs H. Siddons, 44 Heyworth Road, Leicester.**

December 29, 1957.
TRY IT — When serving ice-cream pour ginger wine on top instead of raspberry. It's delicious and can be enjoyed by children as well as grown-ups. — **Mrs H. Kennedy, 89 High Street, Paisley.**

January 26, 1958.
NEW FLAVOUR — When making a jelly, add about a tablespoonful of wine – red for red jellies, sherry to others. It gives the dessert an extra special flavour. — **Mrs A. McMaster, 38 Otago Street, Glasgow.**

January 26, 1958.
WON'T SPOIL — Put a haggis in a covered bowl and cook it as you would a steamed pudding. Then there is no danger of the haggis being spoiled and saturated with water because of the skin bursting. — **Mrs L. Steele, 11 Burnblea Street, Hamilton.**

March 23, 1958.
QUICK SWEET — For an easy pudding when time is limited, pour some hot custard over a swiss roll and heat in the oven.
— **Mrs C. Stevenson, 302 Linthaugh Road, Glasgow.**

August 31, 1958.
LESS WORK — Always add sugar to milk puddings AFTER they are cooked and you have no scorched pans to clean. — **Mrs McPherson, 95 Bellevue Road, Edinburgh, wins a pair of towels.**

October 26, 1958.
NO STICKING — When making steamed puddings, grease the basin, then put a small round of greaseproof paper in the bottom. This prevents the pudding sticking to the basin, and it turns out without breaking. — **Mrs Murdoch, 102 Bank Street, Coatbridge.**

November 30, 1958.
DELICIOUS — Grease pudding basin for plain steamed pudding in the usual way. Shake brown sugar thickly over base and sides. When cooked, this gives the pudding a delicious toffee crust. — **P. Scott, c/o 73 Almond Street, Grangemouth.**

October 4, 1959.
FOR MILK PUDDINGS — Add a pinch of finely-powdered oatmeal to the milk before cooking milk puddings and they turn out much creamier. — **Mrs Davidson, 18½ High Street, Turriff.**

December 20, 1959.
IMPROVES CUSTARD — When making custard, try stirring in a little lemon curd. It not only sweetens, but also gives a delicious flavour. — **Mrs M. M. Kilbride, 57 Whitburn Street, Glasgow.**

Chapter 5

Tarts and Pies

YOUR mother had a lot to do in the house. There was the cleaning, ironing, darning, dusting, blackleading, carpet-beating and gossiping with the neighbours to fit in to her day — which would keep anyone busy enough.

So finding the time to make a tart or a pie didn't happen very often. And, anyway, in the early years of the decade it usually wasn't possible to get the many and varied ingredients for pastry and a filling all together at the same time.

But when the stars aligned...what a lovely treat!

July 30, 1950.

TASTY — Next time you make an apple tart or plate pie, take it out of the oven just before the pastry is ready and sprinkle the top generously with grated cheese. Put back for a few minutes to melt. Spread evenly with a knife. Served either hot or cold, this makes a delicious change. — **Mrs J. Milne, 63 Clouston Street, Glasgow, N.W.**

January 21, 1951.
NO JUICE LOST — When making tarts, wet round the edges with milk instead of water. This seals the sides and keeps all the juices intact. — **Mrs Helen Hare, Melville Cottage, 103 North High Street, Mussselburgh.**

May 13, 1951.
BETTER TARTS — Here's a good tip if you're baking a fruit tart. After lining plate or tin with pastry, sprinkle a good layer of flour and sugar mixed together, then add the fruit. This prevents pastry becoming sodden with juice. — **Mrs R. Barnes, 178 Cuthbertson Street, Glasgow.**

July 15, 1951.
FRUIT — When making fruit pies or tarts, mix a little cornflour with the sugar before adding it to the fruit. This makes the juice like syrup, and prevents it boiling over. — **Mrs L. Niven, 32 Academy Road, Fraserburgh.**

December 9, 1951.
FOR GOOD PASTRY — When making puff pastry to cover a pie, I always fill a lemonade bottle with cold water and use it as a rolling pin. The coolness of the bottle keeps the paste from shrinking when baked, and the pastry is much lighter. — **Mrs M. Macbeth, 29 Hillkirk Street, Springburn, Glasgow, N.**

January 20, 1952.
TART FILLING — When making an open tart, instead of using jam, try the following: Crumble three short biscuits, and mix with two tablespoonfuls of marmalade. Spread this over the usual short crust pastry. — **M. Ritchie, The Villa, Lonmay, Aberdeenshire.**

March 2, 1952.

TART FILLING — To make a lovely fudge filling, put a tin of condensed milk in a pan of water, well covered. Bring to the boil and simmer gently for two hours. Remove tin and when quite cold open it. You'll have a lovely filling for pastry cases. — **M. Gillies, 36 Willowbank Street, Glasgow.**

October 26, 1952.
TARTS — When making a tart, using raw fruit, sprinkle with cornflour as well as sugar. Helps to thicken juice, and prevents boiling over. — **Miss J. Clark, 19 Weir Street, Coatbridge.**

November 14, 1954.
TASTY PIE — When making a meat pie, put a whole onion in the centre. It gives the meat a nice flavour and holds the pastry up beautifully. — **Mrs E. Law, 103 High Street, Renfrew.**

January 30, 1955.
FRUIT TART — When baking a fruit plate tart, line the tin with greaseproof paper. Then the tart can be removed to a wire tray to cool without risk of breakage. — **S. Routledge, 25 Blencowe Street, Carlisle.**

June 19, 1955.
ALWAYS READY — Each week I rub together 3 lb. flour and 1¼ lb. lard and put it in an air-tight tin. I can then, at any time, quickly add water to as much as I need to make a pie or small tarts. – **J. Stoddard, 9 Staveley Road, Ainsdale, Southport, wins a pair of towels.**

March 11, 1956.
CRUMB TOPPING — Add half a cup of rolled oats to brown sugar, butter, and flour for crumb topping for apple or rhubarb tart. It is delicious and crisp. — **Mrs S. Blake, Toolondo, Victoria, Australia.**

November 11, 1956.
FOR FLAVOUR — When making a beef steak pie, get your butcher to cut a marrow bone the depth of your pie dish and use in place of a funnel. This gives a delicious gravy. — **Mrs C. Chambers, 1296 Maryhill Road, Glasgow.**

November 25, 1956.
FANCY PIE — Put your pinking shears to work to make fancy-edged pastry strips for lattice-topped pies or tarts. Dip the blades in flour so they won't stick, and cut the pastry into neat, even strips. — **Mrs H. Tocher, 61 West Church Street, Buckie.**

December 2, 1956.
TARTS — When making apple tarts or fruit pies, sprinkle the sugar on the bottom crust instead of on top of fruit. This sets the juice, there is less chance of it running out, and the bottom of the tart is nice and crisp. — **Miss J. McNaught, High Street, Moniaive, Thornhill.**

January 13, 1957.
SMALL CAKES — When easing fairy cakes, jam tarts, &c., from baking tins, use a grapefruit knife. Being curved, it helps the cakes to come away easily. — **Mrs C. B. Ross, 80 Beaufort Gardens, Bishopbriggs, Glasgow.**

November 10, 1957.
DELICIOUS — When making a baked custard pie, pop a few marshmallows into the pie dish. They rise to the top, melt, and make a delicious meringue. — **Mrs M. Caldwell, 51 Colinslee Drive, Paisley.**

February 9, 1958.
TRIMMING MADE EASY — When covering a steak pie don't go to the bother of cutting off the surplus pastry and putting it on again. Just fold it over and flute it into shape with the handle of a fork or spoon. — **Mrs E. F. Law, 28 Rosalyn Avenue, East Kilbride.**

February 9, 1958.
PASTRY — Always roll out pastry on greaseproof paper. Then it's quite a simple matter to roll paper and pastry up together. Unroll from the top of the pie or on to oven tray. The pastry doesn't stick or break up. — **H. Reid, 24 Dumbarton Road, Clydebank.**

December 21, 1958.
USEFUL SUBSTITUTE — When making an apple pie, if short of a pie funnel, use the core of a large apple covered with sugar for good results. — **Mrs D. Kinnaird, 45 High Street, Edinburgh.**

December 21, 1958.
NO RUNNING OVER — When making fruit pies, put the sugar between two layers of fruit and the juice doesn't boil over.
— Mrs A. Henderson, 12 Woodlands, Turriff.

March 1, 1959.
TRIED AND TESTED — When making small apple tarts, sprinkle the insides of the pastry cases with semolina before putting in previously cooked apples. This absorbs any apple juice and prevents the bottoms of the tarts becoming soggy.
— Mrs H. G. Grant, Hatton Lodge, Hatton, Aberdeenshire.

April 19, 1959.
RHUBARB PIE — Before putting the top on the pie, cut small pieces of a red jelly and mix with the rhubarb. It makes the juice set and also improves the flavour. — **Mrs Cox, 59 Low Road, Balby, Doncaster.**

April 26, 1959.
JAM TARTS — Heat the jam almost to boiling point and the pastry is crisp and not sodden, as it is when cold jam is used. **— Miss A. W. Caw, 19 Falcon Gardens, Edinburgh.**

July 5, 1959.
SUGAR FOR FRUIT — When sweetening fruit such as gooseberries and plums, for tarts or sweets, slit the fruit before stewing. Then the sugar goes through better and you use less. **— Mr W. Mustard, 27 Seafield Street, Cullen.**

August 2, 1959.
TART FILLING — Take two tablespoons marmalade, a piece of butter the size of a walnut and a well-beaten egg. Beat all together until thoroughly mixed. This makes a delicious filling for tarts. **— Miss Walker, 70 Whitehall Road, Drighlington, Bradford.**

September 6, 1959.
MERINGUE PIES — For a clean cut through the meringue, butter the blade of the knife before using. **— Mrs R. Will, 17 Joppa Road, Edinburgh.**

October 4, 1959.
BETTER PASTRY — To prevent the bottom of a fruit flan or tart becoming sodden, brush the pastry with a little beaten egg and leave for a few minutes before putting in the fruit. Next, add a thin layer of uncooked semolina or crushed cornflakes over the pastry and under the fruit. **— Mrs M. Hay, 8 Arnhall Drive, Dundee.**

October 4, 1959.
PIE LIFT — In place of a pie funnel, place a peeled raw onion underneath a slit crust. It will keep the pastry up and gives a lovely flavour. **— Anne Leggatt, 60 Moness Crescent, Aberfeldy.**

Chapter 6

Souper Stuff

WAS there a mother or a grandmother who didn't make soup? Probably not, and thank goodness for that.

On a bitterly cold winter's day there was nothing more welcome than coming home to a bowl of your mum's soup. Was her speciality chicken, ham, beef, onion, pea, tomato or some difficult-to-describe, entirely unique, can-never-quite-be-recreated type of soup she made herself, to her own recipe?

She may have boiled marrowbones, or chicken bones, or a ham hock, and put in barley, lentils, parsley or any one of the things that made her soup unmistakeably hers and only hers.

There was one ingredient common to all the various broths of your childhood, though. No matter what else went into the pot, that soup was made with a lot of love.

May 21, 1950.

BETTER SOUP — When boiling bones for soup, put them on with cold water, as this draws out the nutriment and flavour. Hot water hardens the bones and keeps in the juices. — **Miss N. Gall, 1 Chapel Court, Justice Street, Aberdeen.**

IT'S GOOD TO COME HOME TO
GRANNY'S
TOMATO SOUP
Yes, it's good to come home on cold winter evenings to the warmth of a friendly fire and a piping hot bowl of Granny's Tomato Soup. Everybody looks forward to Granny's Tomato Soup—it's rich—warm—satisfying. Granny's Tomato Soup is so economical, too ! Each can gives you 4 big serves.
GRANNY'S
TOMATO SOUP
SCOTLAND'S FAVOURITE

July 16, 1950.
QUICK THICKENER — If pea or lentil soup seems too thin, add a teaspoonful of vinegar before serving. It will thicken immediately, and won't taste of vinegar. — **Mrs J. Nicol, Gordondale, Port Elphinstone, Inverurie.**

February 15, 1953.
FOR FLAVOUR — When making Scotch broth, add one teaspoon of made mustard and a teaspoon of sugar a half-hour before serving. — **Mrs M. Colville, Kinloch Place, Campbeltown.**

September 20,1953.
FAT REMOVER — To remove fat from cold soup stock, use a flat, perforated fish lifter. It allows stock to drain through, leaving congealed fat on top. — **Mrs M. Dunn, 133 Balornock Road, Glasgow.**

September 12, 1954.
SOFT PEAS — When making split pea soup, the peas become soft in half the usual time if left to cook without salt. Add salt just before serving. — **Mrs W. G. MacRae, 27 Spindlehowe Road, Uddingston.**

September 19, 1954.
SOUP BONES — Bones for soup keep fresh and in good condition for several days if baked for a few minutes in a hot oven. — **Mrs W. Callaghan, Ivy Cottage, Overbrae, Fisherie, by Turriff.**

February 6, 1955.
FATTY SOUP — If the top of your soup looks fatty when simmering, dip a clean cloth in cold water and strain the soup carefully through it. — **C. B. Dickson, 192 Govanhill Street, Govanhill, Glasgow.**

March 30, 1958.
BROTH — When making broth with boiling beef, I always tie the meat in a piece of muslin (previously boiled). It keeps the fat intact, and prevents it breaking up in the soup. — **Mrs J. Middleton, 11 Craigpark Drive, Glasgow.**

December 7, 1958.
SALTY SOUPS — Soups in which bacon or ham bones are boiled are less salty if a whole, peeled potato is added when cooking and removed before serving. — **Mrs M. Dixon, Solway View, Hayton, Nr. Aspatria, Carlisle.**

May 3, 1959.
SOUP — Allow soup to cool before covering it in the pantry. If you cover hot soup it's apt to turn sour. — **Mrs May Falconer, 18 Mair Street, Newmilns.**

May 10, 1959.
SOUP STOCK — When preparing stock for soup, place the bones in a hot oven for quarter of an hour before using. This not only extracts the fat but greatly improves the flavour of the soup. — **Mrs M. Grant, Back Street, Freuchie.**

June 14, 1959.
REMOVING FAT — To remove fat from top of hot soup, place piece of clean greaseproof paper over the surface and dab gently all over. Repeat with more paper until all fat is removed. — **Mrs C. F. McDonald, Duthie Street, Kirriemuir.**

October 4, 1959.
SUBTLE FLAVOURING — To give soups, stews, &c., a nice flavour, try filling a metal tea ball or perforated tea-making spoon with your herbs, onion or bouquet garni. Drop in simmering mixture and remove when flavour suits you. — **Mrs R. Bird, 13X Depot, R.C.A.F. Station, Angus, Ontario, Canada.**

Home-made
soup
and a
hungry
child!
Batchelors
CELERY SOUP
THICK ONION SOUP
MUSHROOM SOUP
OXTAIL SOUP
THICK PEA SOUP
Serve him
Batchelors
Soup Mixes
WITH ALL THE GOODNESS OF HOME-MADE SOUP
What a help these Batchelors Soup Mixes are to your cooking—and there's no better way of making soup for your family!
A packet of Batchelors Soup Mixes gives you all the ingredients you need for home-made soup—specially chosen for flavour and good eating, and all cleaned and ready to cook. You do the cooking yourself, so you know it's freshly cooked with all the goodness and unmistakable flavour of home-made soup.
With 8 varieties to choose from it's easy to give your family different home-made soups every day now. Why not get a couple of packets next time you go shopping?
Chicken Noodle · Celery · French Onion · Thick Vegetable · Mushroom · Oxtail · Thick Onion
Thick Pea

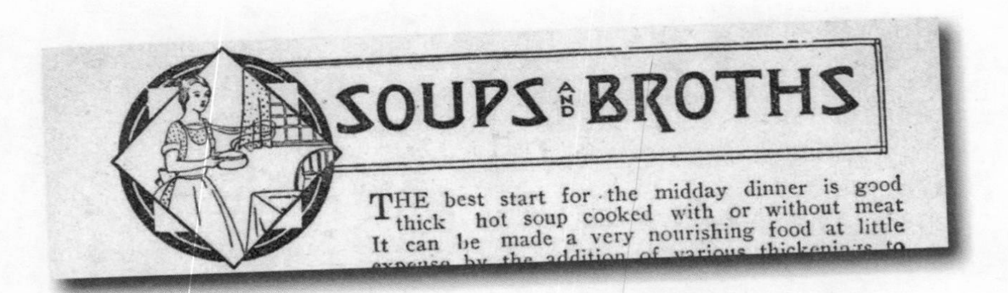

SOUPS AND BROTHS

THE best start for the midday dinner is good thick hot soup cooked with or without meat It can be made a very nourishing food at little

Aunt Kate's hints, tips and recipe pamphlets were given away with magazines and newspapers in the 1950s. This one was a gift with The People's Journal.

Kate would start with sage advice, and let us in on a few secrets of the job, then give recipes.

I recommend all readers try her intriguing Sheep's Head Soup. You only live once.

1950s Pamphlet — The best start for the midday dinner is good thick hot soup cooked with or without meat.

It can be made a very nourishing food at little expense by the addition of various thickenings to meat and vegetable boilings, from beans, peas, potatoes, &c.

There is an art in making good soup, but it is easily acquired if a little care is expended.

An important point is that of slow cooking to enable every ingredient to give its full meed of flavour to the finished article.

Hastily prepared soup is never good. It should be allowed to simmer.

If possible, cooking should be done in a good-sized pan, to prevent waste in boiling over, with tight-fitting lid to keep in all the nourishment.

HOUGH SOUP

1 lb. Hough
4 pints of Water
Salt, Pepper
2 Onions
1 Grated Carrot
1 teacupful Rice

A dish of this soup, piping hot, is much relished on a cold day.

Take 1 lb. hough, wash it, place in a pot and cover with water. Add salt and pepper. Peel the onions and slice finely, add them, and the grated carrot. When the soup has boiled for about 2½ hours, take out hough, separate meat from the bone, cut the meat into pieces and return to the soup, add the rice and boil again for half an hour.

SCOTCH BROTH

1½ lb. Mutton or Beef
2 quarts of Cold Water
1 tablespoonful Barley
1 Onion, 1 Carrot, ½ Turnip
½ dessertspoonful Chopped Parsley
½ teaspoonful Salt
½ teacupful Dried Green Peas
2 or 3 quarts Water

Broth takes a little time to prepare, but it is well worth the trouble for it is the most wholesome and economical dinner fare that you can place on the table.

The quantities given in this recipe will make sufficient soup for a family for two days.

Take 1½ lb. mutton or beef. Put into a pan with the water and salt. Cook gently for 2 hours. Now wash the barley and add to the soup, also the peas, which have been previously soaked, onion, carrot, turnip, and parsley, and cook for 1 hour longer.

SHEEP'S HEAD BROTH

1 Sheep's Head
1 Turnip (large), 2 Carrots, 2 or 3 Leeks
1 teacupful Barley or Rice
Water

HOT SOUPS for COLD DAYS

Soup Don'ts

This is a very nourishing and good soup, which can be made at small cost.

Clean the head and put it into enough cold water to cover it well, add cupful of barley, bring to the boil, skim (if necessary), and add the vegetables cleaned and diced. Simmer gently till the vegetables are cooked — 2 to 3 hours. Lift out the head, take off all pieces of meat, cut up small and add to the soup.

Serve in a hot bowl with potatoes or bread.

LENTIL SOUP

¾ lb. Lentils, ¼ lb. Rice
1 Marrow Bone, Scraps of Cooked or Uncooked Ham
1 Cube Meat Extract
1 Carrot, 1 Onion, ½ Small Turnip
1 teaspoonful Salt
¼ teaspoonful Pepper
3 quarts Water

Lentil soup made the following way is both cheap and nourishing.

To 3 quarts of cold water add the salt and medium-sized marrow bone and any scraps of ham you may have. Let the water heat for five to ten minutes, then add the lentils, rice, carrot (sliced), onion (chopped), turnip, and pepper. Boil gently for four hours. Before removing from the fire add the cube of meat extract.

Stir well and serve.

CLEAR SOUP

1½ lb. Middle Shin of Beef
2½ quarts of Water
2 Carrots, 1 Turnip, 1 Onion
1 tablespoonful Sago, and Seasoning

An excellent soup, and the meat cooked in it may be left over and served for tea or supper.

Put the beef along with the water and vegetables in a pan and simmer together for 3 hours, then add a tablespoonful of sago, previously soaked in water. Boil till clear. Strain and add seasoning. Remove the meat from soup, press between two plates.

Slice and serve cold with salad.

MINCE SOUP

¾ lb. Mince
Small Marrow Bone
Onion, Carrot, Turnip, 3 Leeks
8 Large-Sized Potatoes
2 quarts Cold Water
Seasoning

This is a very tasty soup and a special favourite with children.

Put on the mince and bone with cold water; add the onion and leeks cut up small, also potatoes. Grate carrot and turnip, and simmer for 1½ hours.

SAVOY CABBAGE SOUP

1 Savoy Cabbage
Stock, 2 oz. Rice
½ teacupful Grated Cheese

Try this for a change. It is easy to make and tastes good.

Shred finely a savoy cabbage, put it on to boil in some nicely flavoured stock. Parboil 2 oz. rice. When the cabbage has cooked for 15 minutes throw in rice, let it boil until the rice and cabbage are cooked.

Just before serving add ½ teacupful of grated cheese and serve very hot.

Chapter 7

Keep It Clean

HEALTH & safety legislation and regulations might be regarded as a relatively new phenomena, but it would be a mistake to think of kitchens in the 1950s as dirty.

This was the era of the superhousewife, domestic goddesses and obsessive cleanliness. Our mothers' kitchens were scrubbed, their brasswork rubbed, their silverware polished and their table tops scoured — then scoured again.

And they might not have access to the multitudes of cleaning fluids that line supermarket shelves today, or certificates to hang on the wall claiming they'd attended a 20-minute food handling lesson. They didn't need such things. They kept the hoose clean because that's what their personal standards demanded, and they came up with their own cleanliness regimes to make sure of it.

September 14, 1952.

TINNED FOODS, A WARNING — Tinned foods are generally quite safe. But is your tin-opener? Food-poisoning often arises because the spike of the opener hasn't been cleaned since it was last used, and germs from it get into the food when it punctures the can. — **Mrs R. Watson, Partick, wins a pair of towels.**

September 14, 1952.
COVER UP — When jellies are cooling, be sure to cover with muslin, as gelatin, when exposed to air, attracts dust and germs. **— Mrs G. I. Tyson, 40 Craven Hill Gardens, London.**

September 7, 1952.
FOOD REFUSE — To prevent food refuse adhering to the foot of the refuse bin, line bin with cabbage or rhubarb leaves before using. — **Mrs M. Lawrie, 21 Craigentinny Avenue North, Edinburgh, 6.**

November 23, 1952.
PUDDING CLOTH — Clean a pudding cloth easily by placing it in a saucepan of water with a strip of orange peel. Bring to boil. Peel collects grease and it's then no bother washing out the cloth in warm, soapy water. — **Mrs J. Moran, 826 Duke Street, Glasgow.**

August 15, 1954.
KEEPS FRESH — If you open a jar of meat or fish paste and don't use it all, pour melted butter or margarine on top. This seals the contents and keeps them fresh for a day or two. — **Mrs Isa Anderson, 36 Waverley Park, Bonnyrigg.**

November 14, 1954.
FROSTY VEG — Frosted vegetables should be put into cold water with a teaspoonful of bicarbonate of soda. Let them lie in the water for an hour or so before using. Lift out and wash well, then cook in the usual way. — **Mrs H. Stenhouse, 27 Halliburton Place, Galashiels.**

FOOD NEWS **December 12, 1954.**

Cleaner Food

THOUSANDS of leaflets are to go out to food shops in the next few months. They recommend (amongst other things) that food handlers shouldn't blow into bags, smoke, chew gum, lick their fingers before picking up wrapping paper, or breathe on food.

But – it's "recommended," "suggest," "advise". Eventually, it's "hoped" the recommendations will become law.

Why not now? Reputable firms would welcome such laws. And what a fright other shops would get.

November 2, 1958.
CONDENSED MILK — On opening a tin of condensed milk, pour the contents into a glass jar with a screw top. The milk keeps better and the jar is cleaner to handle than a messy, encrusted tin. — **Mrs N. Inglis, 24 India Street, Montrose.**

April 19, 1959.
EASILY CLEANED — If the juice from apples runs over the oven while cooking, shake salt on it. This causes the juice to burn to a crisp so that it can be easily removed. — **Miss R. Parkhill, 74 Bushmills Road, Coleraine, N. Ireland.**

Chapter 8

Cheesey Does It

CHEESE took a long time to recover from the strictures of rationing. In fact it was the 1990s before some cheeses reappeared. Just before the war, 514 different farms were registered as making cheddar in one small area of England's south-west. In 1974, just 33 farms had re-registered. There was still cheese available in the rationing era, but until 1954 it was "Government Cheese" only. Government Cheese was cheddar, made to an approved recipe with very specific methods. It probably wouldn't have won many cheese-making prizes.

In any case, until the mid 50s when exotic things like sliced cheese came along, most housewives were more worried about how to keep it fresh than what it tasted like.

December 17, 1950.

CHEESE — To keep cheese fresh, wrap it in greaseproof paper then in a bag made of Cellophane or transparent cellulose wrapping. You'll always have a fresh piece of cheese at hand.
— Mrs J. Murray, 10 Cluny Avenue, Bearsden, Glasgow.

October 15, 1950.
CHEESE — Cheese is apt to get hard when kept for a few days. To prevent this, place a slice of lemon alongside it in the dish. It will keep moist much longer. — **Mrs M. H. Stephen, 4 Sunnyside Terrace, Aberdeen.**

July 16, 1950.
CHEESE SLICES — When you want nice thin slices of cheese for sandwiches, use the potato peeler. The pieces are long and thin and don't easily part company with the sandwiches. — **Mrs Parker, 11 Caledonian Crescent, Glasgow W.2.**

April 8, 1951.
CHEESE — A sugar lump in the cheese dish prevents cheese turning mouldy. If you want cheese to keep, wrap it in cheesecloth wrung out in vinegar, repeating as often as the cloth becomes dry. — **L. Gowrie, Bungalow, Spittalfield, Perthshire.**

November 25, 1951.
TASTY — Next time you make an apple tart or plate pie, take it out of the oven just before the pastry is ready and sprinkle the top generously with grated cheese. Put back for a few minutes to melt. Spread evenly with a knife. Served either hot or cold, this makes a delicious change. — **Miss M. McGregor, Sutherland Cottage, Keir Street, Dunblane.**

April 6, 1952.
FRESH CHEESE — Cheese won't dry up if you rub the sliced edge with butter before wrapping it in waxed paper. — **Miss G. Milne, 77 Balvenue Street, Dufftown.**

March 9, 1952.
FLAVOURING — When you add grated cheese to macaroni or scrambled egg, add it only at the last minute. Cheese should always be very lightly cooked. — **Mrs Christina Palmer, 5 Calder Drive, Lochwinnoch.**

FOOD NEWS January 18, 1953.
THE Food Ministry is to buy 1½ million dollars worth of Canadian cheese – about 5 million lb. It will go into the pool.
Continental processed and spreading cheeses are now in the shops in fairly good quantities.

And we may soon get Czechoslovakian blue cheese. A sample order has been received by a Glasgow wholesaler who says it compares very favourably with the Danish kind.

September 20, 1953.
TASTY SPREAD — If cheese has gone hard, grate it into boiling milk, stirring until it becomes thick paste. Add a little salt and allow to cool. — **Miss K. Douglas, 32 Cumlodden Drive, Glasgow.**

March 4, 1956.
CHEESE — To keep cheese from going hard and sweaty, put it (unwrapped) in a polythene bag immediately. It keeps moist and fresh. — **Miss Edith Ross, 67 Arbroath Road, Dundee.**

March 4, 1956.
CLEAN CUT — When cutting soft varieties of cheese, grease the blade of the knife. It then cuts thinly and easily. — **Mrs E. Beaton, 85 Brockburn Road, Glasgow.**

January 20, 1957.
EASY GRATING — To grate bread or cheese to the very end, and also save the fingers, rub it between two graters. — **Miss B. Anderson, 2 Agnew Terrace, Edinburgh.**

FOOD NEWS July 6, 1958.
WHY CHEESE IS A FIRST-CLASS FOOD

DID you know that ounce for ounce, pound for pound, cheese contains more nourishment than any other food? And for less money?

Cheese gives you more protein to build healthy flesh, firm muscle, 230mg. of calcium in every ounce, for strong bones, sound teeth. Doctors tell you to give cheese to growing children, from babyhood on. Old people need cheese, too, to help ageing muscles stay firm.

And, because cheese can't make flabby fat, it helps prevent "middle-aged spread"!

You can't afford to leave cheese out — and at today's prices you can afford to give your family as much as they want of the food they all love.

July 6, 1958.
CHEESE CRAB — To use up that dry cheese, add a drop of vinegar and just a pinch of dry mustard. Mash it into a paste with a fork, soft enough to spread. It's a grand filling for sandwiches.
— Miss Chalmers, 30 Constitution Street, Inverurie.

November 30, 1958.
CHEESE — When using pre-sliced cheese, make a slit in the centre of each square. Insert knife edge and lift. Slices separate more easily. — **Stanley S. McLean, 35 Clune Terrace, Newtonmore.**

January 11, 1959.
CLEAN GRATING — Sprinkle a little semolina on the grater when grating cheese. If it's done frequently, the cheese won't stick. — **Miss N. Cuthbert, 20 Vine Park Avenue, Kilmaurs, Kilmarnock.**

FOOD NEWS July 6, 1958.
STARRED FOR TONIGHT!
A COMPLETELY new way of serving tinned salmon – with cheese. You'll be delighted how delicious it is.

SALMON CHEESE PIE
1 tin salmon: 2 eggs: ½ pint milk: 6 oz. grated Cheddar cheese: pinch cayenne pepper and salt: ½ oz. butter.

Flake the fish carefully and put into a buttered fireproof dish. Beat the eggs, add the milk, grated cheese and seasoning: mix and pour over the salmon. Dot with butter and bake in a very moderate oven (300F. – Gas No. 2) 35 – 45 minutes. Serve hot or cold. 4 servings.

For a fascinating new recipe book, "More Delicious Meals with Cheese," send your name and address (on a postcard, please) to the Cheese Bureau (Dept. F14), 40 Berkeley Square, London, W.1.

October 11, 1959.
TASTY POTATOES — In place of the knob of butter with baked potatoes in their skins, use a knob of one of the many new flavoured spreadable cheeses. Cut the baked potato in two and scoop out a teaspoonful of the flesh and replace with a knob of cheese. This soon melts and soaks down into the potato, giving it a delicious flavour. — **Sonia Y. Hurcombe, 55 Steyning Road, South Yardley, Birmingham.**

December 20, 1959.
NEATER SLICES — When slicing cheese, particularly processed cheese, a good tip is to cover the blade of your knife with greaseproof paper. It slices nicely, and does not break so easily. — **Mrs A. B. Wyatt, 30 Deveron Road, Mastrick, Aberdeen.**

THE British are a nation of cheese-lovers. We have always had livestock in our "green and pleasant land", giving us lots of cow's milk to work with.

But rarely could we be called adventurous. All of the recipes listed here identify "cheese" as the main ingredient — but none stipulate what kind of cheese. It is just . . . cheese.

What we refer to as classic British cheese, firm and yellow or orange, is largely based on a recipe brought over by the Romans, 2,000 years ago — and enjoyed, without much alteration, and described in cooking tips pamphlets that were circulated in the middle of the 20th Century.

Cheese Custard may have fallen out of fashion in recent years, but it might be worth trying...

1950s Pamphlet — Cheese answers nicely the question of how to vary the menu. Why? Because it yields more nutriment, weight for weight or price for price than most other foods.

So housewives who find it difficult to feed a big family on a small income should substitute cheese for meat frequently.

CHEESE AND POTATO PUFF

3 oz. Grated Cheese
¾ lb. Cooked Cold Potatoes
1 Gill Milk
2 Eggs
1 Tablespoonful Butter
Pepper and Salt

This is a delicious savoury for supper, and one that is easily made.

Put the butter and milk into a saucepan, and when hot add the potatoes after rubbing them through a fine sieve; mix thoroughly together over a gentle heat, then add the cheese and cook for another two minutes.

Remove from the fire, season, and add the beaten yolks of the eggs and lastly the stiffly-beaten whites.

Mix well, pour into a buttered pie-dish, and bake for 20 minutes.

Serve hot.

.

CHEESE PUDDING

4 oz. Breadcrumbs
4 oz. Grated Cheese
1 Breakfastcupful Milk
2 Eggs
Pepper and Salt
Mustard, if liked

Any pieces of hard cheese can be used up to make a very appetising pudding thus:

Grate the cheese and add to the breadcrumbs. Heat the milk and pour over. Add seasonings.

Separate the eggs and add the yolks to the mixture. Beat the whites till stiff and fold in gently.

Pour into a greased pie-dish and bake in a hot oven till brown and well risen, usually about 30 minutes.

CHEESE, FISH AND MACARONI

1 lb. of Cooked Fish
¼ lb. Macaroni
1½ oz. of Grated Cheese
½ oz. Butter
Pepper and Salt
¼ pint of White Sauce

Hot, savoury, delicious — try this for to-morrow's dinner and see how everybody likes it.

Remove skin and bone from the fish and separate into flakes. Place the macaroni in boiling salted water and boil for 20 minutes. Drain well.

Make white sauce, add 1 oz. grated cheese, then the fish and macaroni, and mix well together.

Turn the mixture into a buttered pie-dish, sprinkle remaining cheese on top, and bake in a moderate oven for 10 minutes.

CHEESE EGGS

2 oz. Grated Cheese
2 oz. Rice
4 Hard-Boiled Eggs
1 Beaten Egg
1 Finely-Chopped Onion
1 Tablespoonful Tomato Sauce
Breadcrumbs, Parsley, Pepper and Salt
Fat for Frying

Here's a different and most delightful way to serve cheese.

Boil the chopped onion with the rice in a little water until tender and the rice has absorbed all the water; then add the cheese and seasoning and set aside to cool.

Remove the shells from the eggs, divide the rice mixture into four oblong pieces, brush the inside of each piece with tomato sauce, then mould one piece neatly round each egg.

Coat carefully with beaten egg, then breadcrumbs, and fry in boiling fat until golden brown.

Drain, serve hot, garnished with sprigs of parsley.

CHEESE CUSTARD

2 Eggs
1½ Teacups Milk
½ lb. Grated Cheese
1 Teaspoonful Butter
A little Mustard
Salt and Cayenne

You will win new laurels as a clever cook if you serve this dish when visitors come to tea or supper.

Mix all the ingredients well together and bake in a buttered pie-dish for 20 minutes, or steam till custard is set.

WELSH RAREBIT

¼ lb. Cheese
1 oz. Butter
½ oz. Flour
1 Teacupful Milk
1 Egg
Pepper, Salt
Mustard

This is a nice change for six o'clock tea, and it can be made in a few minutes.

Melt the butter, stir in flour and seasoning carefully.

Add milk by degrees, then the cheese (cut in thin slices). Stir till boiling and the cheese has all melted.

Take pan off the fire.

Add the egg and mix thoroughly, and heat again to cook egg.

Spread on buttered toast.

Chapter 9

A Bit Fishy

FISH dishes, of all types, were hugely popular in the 1950s. We ate a lot of it. In 1950, Scotland's fishing fleet comprised 5,222 vessels. By 2016 it was 2,033.

Fish and chips was the universal takeaway of choice — and a real treat. The hot, salt-and-vinegary smell from a chip shop could stop an army in its tracks.

We ate fish at home, too, especially in the rationing years, and there were plenty of techniques, tricks and tips on how best to cook and keep this delicacy...and keep it fresh...and get rid of the smell.

June 4, 1950.

FRESH FISH — If you have to keep fish overnight, lay them flat on an ashet. Wet the paper wrapping with cold water. Put the damp paper on the fish, and sprinkle salt fairly thickly on top of the paper. When the paper is removed next day, the fish will be fresh and stiff. — **Nurse I. A. Wark, Little Deuchar, Fern, by Forfar.**

May 6, 1951.
GOES FURTHER — To eke out a small tin of the best salmon, chop up salmon, grate two good-sized carrots and mix thoroughly. Let stand for 10 minutes before using. The carrots take the taste of the salmon and are not detected. — **Mrs M. Gellatly, 58 Church Street, Dundee.**

September 16, 1951.
NEW WAY WITH COD — As a change, try coating cod cutlets with packet sage and onion stuffing instead of breadcrumbs before frying, and you will enjoy the improved flavour. Serve with fried tomatoes and chips. — **Miss C. McLeod, 160 High Street, Kirkcaldy.**

January 27, 1952.
WHITE AND FIRM — When boiling a thick cut of cod fish, add one tablespoonful of vinegar along with salt to the boiling water. This keeps the fish white and very firm. — **Mrs J. Geddes, Craibstone Cottage, Deskford, Cullen, Banffshire.**

August 3, 1952.
FISHY SMELL — Tea leaves boiled in a fish pan will remove the smell of the fish. — **Mrs J. Nicol, Gordondale, Port Elphinstone, Inverurie.**

February 8, 1953.
COD ROE — Cod roe is in season, but boiling without breaking is a problem. Keep in the paper in which it's wrapped, add another wrapping and put the parcel on to boil. Then the roe is unbroken and tender. — **Mrs J. S. Henderson, 63 Montpelier Park, Edinburgh.**

July 5, 1953.
FRESH FISH — To keep fish fresh in warm weather, cover plate and fish with greaseproof paper and sprinkle cooking salt liberally on top — **Mrs R. Horsham, 289 Maryhill Road, Glasgow.**

August 30, 1953.
FISH DRESSING — Crush a handful of cornflakes and use instead of breadcrumbs when frying fresh fish. Result is lovely golden fish with a delicious flavour. — **Mrs J. S. Ross, Linksfield Cottage, Banff.**

September 27, 1953.
FRYING FISH — Sprinkle the pan with salt to prevent fish sticking to the bottom – and to facilitate turning without breaking the fish. — **Mrs C. Crowe, c/o Cumiskey, 42 Gellatly Street, Dundee.**

December 27, 1953.
FINNAN HADDOCK — If a finnan haddock is smacked on the skin side, then halved (lengthwise) before skinning, the skin comes away without bringing the flesh with it. — **Mrs M. S. Hall, Castle Fraser Flats, Kemnay, Aberdeenshire.**

November 21, 1954.
KIPPERS — To keep kippers from curling up when being cooked, break the bone with a knife in three or four places. The kippers are also more evenly cooked. — **Mrs E. Macleod, Rock House, Wormit.**

November 28, 1954.
FISHY SMELL — To remove the smell of fish from hands, rub fingers with a little dry mustard before washing with soap and water. — **Mrs Thompson, 8 Grange Road, St. Andrews.**

February 20, 1955.
NO WASTE — When sprinkling breadcrumbs over fish, &c., I use a tea strainer. This ensures even distribution and avoids waste. — **Mrs M.B. Tawse, 19 Glamis Drive, Dundee.**

May 22, 1955.
COD STEAKS — When frying cod steaks tie a piece of white thread around them. This keeps them firm and easier to serve. — **Miss W. Johnstone, 2 Linskill Villas, St Andrews.**

June 26, 1955.
KEEPS FISH FRESH IN HOT WEATHER — To keep fish fresh for a day or two in hot weather, line a dish with greaseproof paper which has been lightly sprinkled with salt. Place a layer of fish, cover with more paper and a thin layer of salt. Do this until dish is full, finishing with a layer of salt. — **Mrs A. McIntosh, 759 Maryhill Road, Glasgow, wins a pair of towels.**

February 12, 1956.
CLEAN FAT — When frying fish in deep fat, place a piece of muslin inside fish basket. This keeps the fat free from crumbs. — **H. Parker, 6 Bowmanflat, Larkhall.**

April 29, 1956.
BATTER — When making batter for frying fish, meat, &c., add a teaspoonful olive oil. This gives the batter extra crispness. — **Mrs Jackson, Carlisle.**

February 10, 1957.
EASY FILLETING — I find when I fillet fish it makes the job easier if I dip my fingers in a little fine salt. It helps to get a firm hold, and the job is done in half the time. — **Mrs D. Nicolson, Greenlea, Castletown, Caithness.**

March 3, 1957.
FISH BATTER — When making batter for fish, add ¼ teaspoonful dry mustard, and leave for about an hour before using. This makes a tasty change from the usual plain flour. — **Mrs I. Anderson, 36 Waverley Park, Bonnyrigg.**

October 26, 1958.
CRISP BATTER — Add a pinch of bicarbonate of soda to the batter prepared for fish. Cook in deep fat, and it turns out lovely and crisp. — **Mrs H. Locher, 2 Coastguard Station, Leven.**

May 17, 1959.
FRIED FISH — Instead of serving slices of lemon with the fish, try adding finely-grated lemon rind to the flour used for the batter. It gives the fish a delicious flavour — **Mrs C. Gan, c/o 83 Belvedere Court, Dryburgh Road, Putney, London.**

July 19, 1959.
HERRINGS — Dip fresh herrings and mackerel in vinegar before coating with seasoned oatmeal. This makes them nice and crisp and takes away any excessive greasiness. — **Mrs J. Scott, Benholm, Montrose.**

August 23, 1959.
KEEPS FLIES AWAY — A sprig of fresh mint laid over meat or fish will keep flies away in warm weather until the food is ready to be cooked. — **Mrs Telford, 78 Central Avenue, Grangemouth.**

November 8, 1959.
KIPPERS — Before serving kippers or fried fish, cover each plate with a circle of greaseproof paper. If this paper is rolled up carefully afterwards, there's no fishy grease and no bones on the plates. — **Miss B. S. Mackechnie, 13 Craigmuschat Road, Gourock.**

Chapter 10

Fruity

THE most remarkable thing about fruit in the 1950s was that, for a lot of the time, there wasn't much of it.

Like all things to do with food, rationing was to blame. But, scarcities or not, there was a fairly narrow (by today's standards) range of fruits we wanted. There wasn't much demand for mangoes, kumquats or Goji berries. Such outlandish things hadn't made much of a dent on the British market. It must be acknowledged, however, that expert and inventive housewives would have performed miracles with them, if they'd had them. Just reading their tips for fruit tells you that.

Coconuts and figs (usually dried) was about as exotic as it got. Prunes, rhubarb and (regrettably) gooseberries were more readily available.

In the early 1950s, though, there was a lot of attention given to bananas. Or, rather, the lack of bananas. They had been widely available before 1939, but many people didn't fully accept the war was over until there were bananas in shops again.

February 8, 1953.
DATES — Dates which have gone hard and sugary are soft and palatable again if wrapped in muslin and steamed for half an hour.
— Mrs E. Morrans, 28 Dalaruan Terrace, Campbeltown.

January 4, 1953.
WHOLE NUTS — To get nuts out of their shells in one piece, soak them in salt and water for a few hours. — **Miss D. MacGregor, Sutherland Cottage, Dunblane.**

January 11, 1953.
PRUNES — To take away the sweetness of prunes, add a strip of lemon peel while cooking. — **Miss Wilson, Welfare Grounds, Fulwell Road, Sunderland.**

FOOD NEWS January 18, 1953.
THERE will be plenty oranges in the shops this week, some a little cheaper.

Apples — from about 1s to 2s a lb. Tomatoes 1s 9d to 2s 2d a lb. South African pears 1s 9d to 2s a lb. Peaches 1s to 1s 6d each. Plums 1s 8d to 2s 6d a lb.

Forced rhubarb is down in price by about 3d (1s to 1s 3d a lb.). Sprouts more plentiful (and cheaper) at 6d to 9d a lb. Carrots 3d to 4d a lb. Cauliflower 1s to 1s 6d each. Onions are a little dearer at about 9d a lb.

March 29, 1953.
FIGS — Dried figs are often tough after cooking. To prevent this, soak in cold water for 48 hours. They're then ready for using. No sugar is required. — **Mrs M. L. Stobie, 7 Sutherland Road, Tunbridge Wells.**

May 24, 1953.
COOL DRINK — Beat a banana and one teaspoonful sugar to a pulp in a tumbler and fill up with cold milk. — **Mrs W. Dickie, 11 Loganlea Gardens, Edinburgh.**

January 10, 1954.
CHERRIES — If glace cherries have become damp and sticky, put them in an airtight jar with a little castor sugar. This not only restores them, but improves the flavour and appearance.
— **Mrs E. Dunsmuir, 34 Taymouth Street, Glasgow.**

February 7, 1954.
PRUNES — Add a dessertspoonful of treacle when stewing prunes. It darkens the syrup and enhances the flavour.
— **Mrs L. Corke, Glenboyne, Cornhill, Banffshire.**

April 25, 1954.
BANANAS — To prevent bananas turning black and soft, store in a pan with a tight-fitting lid. — **Mrs R. Parnaby, 41 Howard Street, North Shields.**

June 20, 1954.
IT HELPS TO KEEP LEMONS FRESH — Lemons will quickly deteriorate once they've been cut. Place cut parts in a saucer with a few drops of vinegar, and it keeps fresh longer.
— **Mrs M. Buchahan, 26c Weir Street, Stirling, wins a pair of towels.**

April 24, 1955.
WALNUTS — Chopping walnuts with a knife is a tedious job. Instead, place them between a fold of greaseproof paper and press gently with the rolling-pin. — **Mrs D. Stark, Dalshian, 55 Midton Road, Prestwick.**

March 4, 1956.
HANDY STRAINER — After squeezing juice from lemons I always use a tea strainer to catch the pips. It saves time when making a hot drink, &c. — **Mrs Rankin, 6 Woodside Crescent, Auchenback, Barrhead, Glasgow.**

May 20, 1956.
LEMONS — Before grating lemons, cleanse them of any small brown specks on the outside peel by soaking in cold water for 20 minutes. Then rub with a vegetable brush. — **Miss R. Lock, 84 Watermoore Road, Cirencester.**

June 3, 1956.
RHUBARB — Don't stew rhubarb in water. Cut it up and cover with sugar overnight. Cook in its own juice next day. It then retains its full flavour. — **Miss J. Rizza, 45 Seafield Street, Cullen.**

December 9, 1956.
ALMONDS — I find it easier to remove almond skins by soaking overnight in water. The skins come off easily without toughening the nuts. — **Mrs C. Henderson, 78 Urquhart Road, Aberdeen.**

January 20, 1957.
APPLES — Apples that are dried up and skins withered need not be wasted. Place them in cold water overnight. They're freshened and firm in the morning. — **Miss Rizza, Seafield Street, Cullen.**

March 10, 1957.
EASY SLICING — If you are slicing bananas for the top of a cake or salad, use an egg slicer. It gives neat, uniform pieces. — **Mrs L. Kennedy, 11 Balgraybank Street, Glasgow.**

March 31, 1957.
IMPROVES FLAVOUR — When cooking apples or rhubarb I always add a pinch of salt. It keeps the colour of the fruit and improves the flavour. — **Miss A. C. Robertson, 250 Dalry Road, Edinburgh.**

April 7, 1957.
APPLES — Pour boiling water over apples and leave for a few minutes. The skins can then be removed easily and without waste. **— J. Simpson, 92 Hepburn Gardens, St Andrews.**

July 7, 1957.
SUMMER TREAT — Cut a banana into slices. Melt a bar of plain chocolate, coat the banana slices, and then roll them in coconut. Delicious! — **Miss J. Leuchars, Balnacraig, Dunain, Inverness.**

September 15, 1957.
COOKING APPLES — Boil the water and sugar slowly for about 15 minutes, then add the sliced apples, and simmer. They don't break — and they taste delicious. — **Mrs A. E. Hendry, 6 Avenue Crescent, Leeds.**

February 2, 1958.
THRIFTY — When making apple tarts or stewed apples, don't throw the skins and cores away. Wash and stew them, sweeten and strain. The syrup, served with plain sponge puddings and trifles, is delicious, and every part of the apple is used. — **Mrs L. Ross, 47b Carlingwark Street, Castle Douglas.**

June 29, 1958.
SUMMER SWEET — A delicious way of serving rhubarb for anyone who cannot take it in its usual form is to cut a red jelly over the top of the rhubarb in a casserole. Cook slowly with lid until tender. No sugar or water required. Serve with cream on top when cold. — **Miss Imlach, The Elms Hotel, Dufftown.**

July 6, 1958.
COOKING FRUIT — Fruit is improved in flavour and much less likely to break in cooking if it is cooked in a covered casserole or fireproof dish in a moderate oven. — **Mrs Charlotte Gibson, 112 Stirling Road, Larbert.**

September 7, 1958.
APPLES — When a recipe says peel and core apples, always core before peeling. The apples won't break as they often do when peeled first. — **Mrs W. Gillies, 100 Den Walk, Methil.**

September 21, 1958.
APPLE SAUCE — To give apple sauce more interest, add a dessertspoonful of cooking sherry and a dash of grated nutmeg. **— Mrs H. McNaughton, 13 Cromwell Road, Rugby.**

March 1, 1959.
NON-STICKY — When you buy loose glace cherries, empty them into a glass jar with a screwtop. Dredge them well with ground rice and shake up in the jar. When you require them, they are quite dry and separate. — **Mrs E. J. Foster, 4 North Road, Tow Law, Co. Durham.**

March 15, 1959.
TOFFEE APPLES — When making toffee apples, put a stick at each end. It is much easier for children to hold. — **Mrs W. Stewart, 51 Cairndhuna Terrace, Wick.**

July 12, 1959.
EASIER SANDWICHES — When making date sandwiches and you find the stoned date blocks a bit hard, place the sealed packet in a basin of hot water for a few minutes. This makes the dates soft and easy to spread. They go further, too. — **J. Dickie, 2 Kilbourne Terrace, Bellshill.**

August 16, 1959.
BOTTLED PEARS — To give bottled pears a professional look after peeling and halving, scoop out the cores with a teaspoon. This leaves a smooth dent the shape of the spoon and takes much less time than digging out with a knife. — **Mrs G. Hadden, 3 Neville Terrace, Priestgate, Peterborough.**

August 30, 1959.
STORING APPLES — Cardboard egg cartons make excellent stands for storing apples. It is sometimes necessary to use alternate egg spaces according to size of apples. Cover with greaseproof paper. — **M. Taylor, c/o Greig, Whitehills, Forfar.**

October 25, 1959.
APPLES — When storing cooking apples for winter use, rub palms of hands with Vaseline, roll apples in hands, then wrap in tissue paper. Skins of apples don't shrivel up. — **Mrs G. Cruickshank, 66 Hillfield Road, Inverkeithing.**

December 6, 1959.
NUTS — Remove Brazil nuts whole by putting them in water and bringing to the boil. Then crack in the normal way. — **Mrs H. Dale, 70 Manuel Street, Goole.**

December 13, 1959.
ADD SHERRY — Next time you are serving fruit salad and cream, add a few drops of sherry to the cream before whipping. It's delicious! — **Mrs W. Callaghan, The Bungalow, Cardow Distillery, Knockando.**

December 20, 1959.
ICE CUBES — If you have a fridge and like to keep ice cubes for drinks, they look very decorative with tinned cherries or other fruit popped into each cube before freezing. Adds flavour, too. — **Mrs J. McWhirter, 6 Mayfield Road, Saltcoats.**

December 20, 1959.
APPLE TIP — When peeling apples, have at hand a basin of cold water to which a few drops of lemon juice have been added. As the apples are peeled drop them into the water, and they keep their fresh colour. — **Mrs J. Farren, 47 Seedhill Road, Paisley.**

Chapter 11

Rapid Recipes

EXPECTATIONS for the food we prepared became ever more ambitious during the decade of the 1950s. As the years went by, the concept of finding new and interesting recipes grew.

There were previously unknown foodstuffs coming on the market and the social make-up of Britain became more diverse, so attitudes to food changed. Women like Elizabeth David were writing cookbooks telling of exotic ingredients like aubergines and olive oil.

Home cooks became more confident about sharing ideas and expertise and the exchanging of recipes between ordinary people became fashionable. Most were simple, but then there wasn't room on newspaper and magazine pages for lengthy lists of instructions — and who says recipes have to be complicated, anyway?

This chapter is one that, I hope, you'll come back to again and again. What was that Viennese Shortcakes recipe that Mrs Wright, of Dunfermline, recommended in 1959...?

December 31, 1950.

MOCK CHICKEN — Cut a rabbit into nice sizes pieces. Dip each piece in well-seasoned flour. Put into a casserole, and put a few small onions round it. Sprinkle half a cup of soft breadcrumbs with sage and chopped parsley added. Lastly, pour over a cup of milk and cook in a slow oven for 2½ hours, with the lid on.
— Mrs Kelly, 48 Middleton Avenue, Uphall, Broxburn.

September 30, 1951.
DELICIOUS — Here's a sweet that needs no milk — and is very easy on sugar. Boil a pint of water in a pan, add a table jelly, and keep stirring until completely dissolved. Gradually add two good tablespoonfuls of semolina and one tablespoon sugar. Simmer gently for 15 minutes, stirring often. Turn into bowl, and, when cold, beat vigorously until the mixture becomes light and fluffy. Enough for four persons. — **Mrs Mollie Watson, The Chalet, Culloden Moor, Inverness-shire.**

October 19, 1952.
TOPICAL TIP — I've just made three good dinners (for two) — and a "piece" — for 1s! The shilling bought 1 lb. jointed rabbit. I floured the joints and fried them in margarine with a sliced onion; put rabbit and onion in a casserole, dusted it with a little powdered thyme, poured rich gravy over, and put in oven until tender. I find this enough for two days. I still had a little meat over and some liver. The liver was chopped and, mixed with a relish, provided the "piece." Scraps of meat were minced, mixed with a good white sauce, put in pastry cases — and made four "chicken" patties for the third dinner — **Mrs M. Murison, 34 Hutcheon Street, Aberdeen.**

October 25, 1953.
NO APPETITE? — Try sipping this drink. Beat an egg yolk with a spoonful of honey. Stir in juice of an orange and put into a tumbler. Fill up with milk and finally add the stiffly beaten white of an egg. — **Mrs R. H. Paterson, 369 Knightswood Road, Knightswood, Glasgow.**

November 11, 1956.
NEW FILLING — Put eight or ten marshmallows in a basin and stand over boiling water till melted to a cream. Cream together 1 oz. margarine and 1 oz. castor sugar till light and fluffy. Then beat in the cooled and melted mallows, and use for sponge cake filling. — **Mrs L. Waugh, 18 Wardlaw Street, Edinburgh.**

January 5, 1958.
QUICK SNACK — A quick supper dish, tasty but inexpensive, is made by mixing thoroughly — 3 tablespoons S.R. flour, 1 beaten egg, ¾ cupful milk, salt and pepper, and a small tin of baked beans. Drop spoonfuls into boiling deep fat and cook till nicely browned. — **Miss E. M. Brown, 11 Murison Drive, Rosehearty, Aberdeenshire.**

February 23, 1958.
CHOCOLATE CUPS — To make your own chocolate cups, use slab chocolate (the kind sold for cake-covering) and some fluted, greaseproof paper cases. Melt the chocolate in the oven until runny, but not hot. Pour into cases a little at a time and run it evenly with a knife, coating the entire case. Leave till hard, then tear the paper gently away from the chocolate.
— **Mr Brydon, Greenhaugh, Insch, Aberdeenshire.**

August 3, 1958.
STARRED FOR TODAY! — Watch the family's faces when you put this dish on the table. It looks and tastes like a million dollars, yet, with cheese and eggs so wonderfully low-priced, it's really economical! And you'll find that cheese soufflé is not nearly so difficult to prepare as most people think! — 1 oz. butter; ½ oz. plain flour; ¼ pt. milk; 3 oz. grated Cheddar cheese; 3 eggs (separated); A good pinch of salt; pepper; 1 extra egg-white. Melt the butter in a saucepan, add flour and cook slowly, stirring, for about a minute. Draw the pan to one side and gradually mix in the milk. Stir as you bring to the boil. Cook a few minutes. Remove pan from heat, add grated cheese, seasoning. Beat in the egg yolks, one at a time. Cool the sauce and fold in stiffly beaten egg whites. Pour into a greased 7-inch soufflé case or deep fireproof dish. Bake in the middle of a moderate oven (350°F. – Gas No. 4) for 35 minutes. Serve at once.

August 3, 1958.
QUICK WELSH RAREBIT — Sizzling Welsh Rarebit is a dish nobody ever gets tired of! And here's a wonderful new way to make it that takes very little time. Cut a thick slice of Cheddar cheese, and put it on a piece of toast under the grill. In a minute you'll have a glorious, golden-toasted Welsh Rarebit — a hot dish fit for a king!

August 24, 1958.
BACON AND TOMATO FONDUE — Trim 8 rashers of bacon and fry till crisp. Now, fry 8 fingers of bread in the bacon fat and put them into a shallow fireproof dish, covering each piece with a rasher of bacon. Slice 8 tomatoes and place them on top of the bacon. Put the dish in a warm place while you prepare a fondue sauce, like this: grate 12 oz. of Cheddar cheese and put with 6 tablespoonfuls of milk, a few drops of Worcester sauce, cayenne pepper and salt into a small pan and heat very carefully, stirring gently, until the cheese melts. Add 2 well beaten eggs to the sauce and continue to stir over a very low heat until the sauce thickens. Pour the sauce over the bacon and tomato fingers and serve at once. (4 servings, approximate cost 5/3.)

September 14, 1958.
TEA-TIME TREAT — Tempting tea-time dainties can quickly be made by sandwiching two butter puff biscuits with jam and mock cream with icing on top. — **R. Gordon, 3 Houldsworth Street, Glasgow.**

January 11, 1959.
SAVOURY — When cooked, mash suede turnip with margarine and an egg yolk. Place in a greased casserole and top with stiffly beaten egg white into which have been folded two tablespoonfuls grated cheese, pinch of salt and cream of tartar. Brown in moderate oven. — **Mrs E. Stewart, 22 Harvard Road, Chiswick, London.**

February 1, 1959.
A TREAT — Toast as many slices of bread as you require — on one side only. Butter the untoasted side. Put a teaspoonful of grated cheese and an egg yolk on each buttered side. Add the stiffly-beaten white on top of the yolk, and another tablespoonful of cheese to finish off. Cook in a moderate oven until the meringue is firm and the cheese browned. — **Mrs E. Strang, 73 Almond Street, Grangemouth.**

February 8, 1959.
NEW SUPPER DISH — For a change, instead of just reheating a tin of spaghetti, following directions given, break three whole eggs over the contents of two small tins (or one large). Sprinkle one teaspoonful curry powder and stir the whole mixture over heat until eggs are cooked. Add salt to taste. This makes a delicious supper dish for four people. — **Miss R. Ishak, 2 Drumsheugh Gardens, Edinburgh, wins a pair of towels.**

February 8, 1959.
TASTY DISH — Crush a packet of potato crisps and mix them with grated cheese. Put on top of a dish of creamed fish, and pop back into oven. This makes a good topping. — **Miss L. Murdoch, 45 Wheatlands Avenue, Bonnybridge.**

March 8, 1959.
VIENNESE SHORTCAKES — 2 oz. icing sugar, 3 oz. marg., 4 oz. flour. Cream icing sugar and marg. together, then add flour. Place teaspoonfuls of mixture on greased tray and mark with fork. Bake in slow oven for about 25 minutes. When cool, put together with a little butter icing. — **Mrs S. Wright, 140 Arthur Street, Dunfermline.**

April 26, 1959.
RETAINS FLAVOUR — Put rhubarb into a small pudding bowl after washing and cutting into small pieces. Add sugar, but not water. Put bowl into a pan of cold water to come half-way up the bowl. Put on lid and cook slowly till ready. — **Mrs Martin, 28 Killearn Street, Glasgow.**

June 21, 1959.
EXTRA NICE — To make a specially good custard, make as usual and, when a little cool, empty in a small tin of unsweetened evaporated milk and beat well. It's delicious. — **Mrs C. Bain, 64 East Barn Street, Clydebank.**

July 5, 1959.
TOPPING THE TARTS — To make glaze for strawberry tarts, blend 1 rounded teaspoonful strawberry-flavoured cornflour and 1 heaped teaspoonful sugar with a little water taken from ¼ pint water. Heat remainder and make as for cornflour. Allow to cool, then pour over strawberries. **— Mrs Irene Meiklejohn, Avondale, Touch Road, Cambusbarron.**

September 27, 1959.
SAVOURY DISH — Line buttered pie-dish with 1 lb. sliced cooked potatoes, season with salt, pepper and dry mustard. Sprinkle 3 oz. chopped cooked ham on top. Empty small tin evaporated milk into a pan with 6 oz. shredded cheese and melt over slow heat. Pour over contents in pie-dish and cook half an hour in moderate oven. — **Mrs M. A. Lyle, 116 Wood Street, Galashiels.**

October 4, 1959.
PARTY FARE — Top crumpets with grated cheese then slices of tomato. Top with anchovy fillets or sardines and season with salt and pepper. Bake in moderate oven for 10 to 15 minutes. **— Mrs E. Higgs, 70 Dent Street, Glen Iris, S.E.6, Victoria, Australia.**

October 4, 1959.
TASTY DISH — Mix half a packet of soup powder, mushroom flavoured, with one teacupful milk and boil to the consistency of thick sauce. Add a potato well mashed and unsalted and ¼ lb. of cooked beef cut in small pieces. Place in well greased dish, sprinkle with breadcrumbs and small piece of butter and bake until nicely browned on top. — **E. Evans, 6 Hay Place, Edinburgh.**

October 11, 1959.
NEW WAY WITH PRUNES — Prunes in cider are tasty for a treat. No cooking is required. You simply pack prunes in screw-top jar and pour cider over them. Screw on the lid firmly and leave until prunes absorb most of the cider. Not for immediate use, of course! — **Mrs A. Low, East Hill Brae Cottages, Brechin.**

November 1, 1959.
QUICK SUPPER SNACK — Toast round slices of bread on one side. Spread mustard on untoasted sides and place on each a slice of ham, top with a slice of pineapple, sprinkle with brown sugar and pop under the grill until hot. — **Mrs E. Higgs, St John's Wood, off Grantulla Road, Kallista, Victoria, Australia.**

November 29, 1959.
RAINBOW CAKE — This can be made using one bowl only. Spoon part of the mixture into a prepared tin. Colour the rest pink and put half in the tin, followed by the remainder, to which melted chocolate has been added. Score with a knife for rainbow effect. — **Mrs G. H. Wayman, 92 King's Road, Harrogate.**

December 6, 1959.
ORANGE SWEET — Allow one orange per person. Peel and slice with serrated-edged knife. Put slices in bottom of dish, sprinkle with caster sugar and then a generous helping of desiccated coconut. Continue in this way until bowl is filled up. It can be served straight away, but the flavour is improved if allowed to stand for a while. — **Mrs Travis, 63 Dale Road, Barnard Castle.**

December 20, 1959.
NEW SWEET — Cut a vanilla ice-cream brick into six slices and top each with this syrup — put 1 oz. of roughly-chopped crystallised ginger into a saucepan, add 4 tablespoons of water and 1 tablespoon syrup. Heat together for several minutes and then leave to get cold. — **Miss B. Fisher, 23 Belham Road, Peterborough.**

December 20, 1959.
TASTY DISH — Stew ½ lb. mince with onion and browning. Strain gravy from mince and allow to cool. Chop 3 oz. suet finely and add to 6 oz. flour and pinch of salt. Mix to stiff consistency with milk and water. Roll out rather thinly and spread mince over. Make into roly-poly, closing ends securely and bake in a crisp oven until nicely browned. Cut in slices and pour thickened gravy over when serving. — **Mrs E. Evans, 6 Hay Place, Edinburgh.**

Chapter 12

Tea With Milk

THINK of your mother or grandmother in their house. Think of them chatting, think of them solving their own, their family's and the world's problems. Chances are, you picture them making or drinking a cup of tea.

Tea was oil on troubled water. Tea was a time to talk. Tea was the first thing made on a cold morning and the last thing taken to wash down supper.

And there was milk always at hand in the 1950s. It was delivered to the doorstep, it was used in an awful lot of recipes and it was an integral part of a brew up.

You'd think, then, that there would be more tips about tea than anything else. But tea with milk was so common that it wasn't discussed any more than the human body's need for oxygen was discussed or the fact that gravity made things knocked off a table fall down. A cuppa was just..."there".

July 16, 1950.

WON'T TASTE — To prevent the queer taste a new aluminium teapot sometimes gives the tea, put in a few crushed eggshells and fill with boiling water. When cold, wash and rinse with boiling water. — **Mrs B. Thomson, Heiton Village, Kelso.**

July 23, 1950.
FRESH MILK — Mix waterglass to double strength (using only half the amount of water stated in the directions). Put the mixture in a pail and set in it your uncapped bottle or milk jug, making sure none of the mixture enters the milk. This prevents milk going sour. The mixture lasts as long as any heatwave is likely to last. — **James Gillan, 24 The Valley, Stenhousemuir.**

July 22, 1951.
CLEAN POTS — Aluminium teapots get very brown inside with constant use. To clean, put a teaspoonful of borax in the pot, fill up with hot water, and leave all night. When rinsed out in the morning, the pot will be perfectly clean. The same method can be applied to saucepans and other aluminium utensils. — **Mrs Ronald, 179 Hilton Avenue, Aberdeen.**

July 27, 1952.
COFFEE — A pinch of mustard added to the boiling water when making coffee will soften the water and bring out the true flavour of the coffee. — **Jean Marshall, 30 Staffa Street, Glasgow.**

February 20, 1955.
TEA TIP — Pour five cupfuls of water into a saucepan. Bring to the boil. Add one teaspoonful of tea and boil for three minutes. Tip the brew into the teapot, and it is ready for use. Try this and you won't go back to the old expensive, wasteful method.
— Mrs J. W. Brown, 12 Danube Street, Edinburgh.

April 3, 1955.
DUST-FREE MILK — An inverted plastic egg-cup makes an excellent milk bottle top. Keeps out all dust and is easy to handle.
— J. M. Hill, 119 Restalrig Road South, Edinburgh.

September 9, 1956.
SOUR MILK — If you have no sour milk when the recipe calls for some, use sweet milk and add two tablespoonfuls vinegar to each cup required. — **Mrs Wm. Graham, 79 Faskine Avenue, Cairnhill, Airdrie.**

December 16, 1956.
MILK — When milk is almost boiling over drop a spoon into the pan, and it keeps the milk from rising. — **Mrs M. Murdoch, 54 Chesser Crescent, Edinburgh.**

May 5, 1957.
MILK — To help prevent milk from turning sour in hot weather, stand the bottles on a layer of coarse kitchen salt in a suitable container (not tin), and place in a shady, cool place. — **M. Whiteside, 83 Aitkenhead Avenue, Coatbridge.**

November 22, 1959.
BUTTER ECONOMY — Beat up a pound of butter with half a pint of slightly-warmed milk, beating just long enough to mix in all the milk. The butter goes farther when treated in this way. — **Mrs H. Tocher, 2 Coastguard Station, Promenade, Leven, wins a pair of towels.**

Chapter 13

The Fat Of The Land

NOWADAYS, fat is just about Public Enemy No. 1. Virtually every food label in the supermarket shouts about how much fat it hasn't got.

Somehow, over the years, fat went out of fashion.

It used to be sought after. There was a limit to the amount of fat you could get. The ration book had a lot to say about the amount of lard you were entitled to. Because fat made tasty things. And it filled you up.

I have to add that, on a personal note, fat formed a major part of my favourite childhood food.

When the mince or stew was cooking, my mother skimmed the fat off the top and poured it on a piece of bread until the bread was soggy and sodden through with glistening, glutinous, delicious fat. This delicacy was titled "a piece and dip".

It was truly wonderful. I have tried many times to recreate it but my modern-day efforts never match that meaty, salty, fatty, runny, magical taste.

If I somehow discovered how to travel in time, going back to take careful notes on how a proper piece and dip was created would be the first task on my list.

Cookeen
REAL FAT, GOOD AND RICH
The pure rich fat
for the 'Golden Touch'

August 13, 1950.
IF YOU'RE BOTHERED WITH SPARKING FAT — Turn a colander upside down over frying fish or meat. The small holes allow steam to escape, but keep grease from spattering about. **— Mrs M. Cormack, 24 Devon Street, Barrow-in-Furness, wins this week's guinea.**

June 3, 1951.
PRECIOUS FAT — Before frying bread, pop it under the grill to dry off for a few seconds. When treated this way before immersing in the hot fat, the bread starts to brown immediately and does not absorb so much fat. — **Mrs D. E. Macarthur, 10 Hawksmoor Road, Rising Brook, Stafford.**

October 5, 1952.
SUET — Melt down butcher's suet like other fat. Strain into a mould and allow to set. Grate off amounts as required. Suet so treated will keep fresh indefinitely. — **J. T. Nelson, 27 Becketts Park Drive, Leeds.**

October 26, 1952.
SUET — Suet will remain good for a time if buried in sufficient flour to exclude air. A bag of flour is suitable. — **Mrs W. Johnston, 15 Thorndale Avenue, Larne, Co. Antrim.**

August 1, 1954.
KEEPS FAT CLEAN — When frying fish in deep fat, place a muslin cover inside the fish basket. This will keep the fat free of crumbs. — **Mrs Johnston, 63 Port Dundas Road, Glasgow.**

April 29, 1956.
SAUSAGES — Fry sausages in the chip pan in deep fat. This browns them more evenly and quickly, and there's no sparking fat. **— Mrs R. Pringle, 55 Clayport Gardens, Alnwick.**

November 18, 1956.
FAT — A quick and efficient way to clarify fat is to line a strainer with fine white cotton material. Hold the strainer over a basin and pour in the hot fat. You will have lovely clear fat all ready for use. — **Mrs B. Baxter, 70 Garthdee Drive, Aberdeen.**

December 9, 1956.
EASY BASTING — Fill a muslin bag with shredded suet, herbs, and seasoning, and tie it to the bars above the baking pan on which the roast is placed. When the oven gets hot, the fat and seasoning drips on to the joint and keeps it basted continually. — **Mrs C. Black, 20 Springvalley Gardens, Edinburgh.**

February 24, 1957.
WHEN BAKING — If the hands are rubbed over with lard before kneading bread or making pastry, the mixture doesn't stick to them. — **Mrs F. Wear, 69 Aisthorpe Road, Sheffield.**

May 5, 1957.
SANDWICHES — Left over sandwiches need not be thrown out. They are delicious deep fried in fat and served hot. — **Mrs F. W. Bell, 18 Westlands, Chester Road, Sunderland.**

November 17, 1957.
SUET — Sprinkle suet with flour and put through the mincer. It is quicker and better than chopping. — **M. Rogan, 25 Dunelm Road, Trindon Village, County Durham.**

November 9, 1958.
FRYING FAT — If your frying fat becomes slightly burnt, drop a raw potato into the pan and leave for ten minutes or so. It absorbs the burnt taste. — **Mrs J. Smith, 30 Rosetta Place, Peebles.**

May 3, 1959.
SUET — When chopping suet, sprinkle with a little ground rice. It chops more easily and doesn't stick to the knife. — **Miss F. Kennedy, 89 High Street, Paisley.**

July 12, 1959.
NEW FLAVOUR — When heating baked beans add a teaspoonful of roast or pork dripping. This not only thickens the juice, but adds a new flavour to the beans. — **Mrs M. Simpson, 80 Ardgowan Street, Glasgow.**

November 22, 1959.
SUET — When suet is short, sago soaked in milk or water until quite soft does just as well. — **Mrs A. MacLeod, West End, Glenglass, Evanton.**

Chapter 14

Very Good Vegetables

THERE weren't many vegetarians in the 1950s but there was a lot of vegetables, often grown at home. This was an extension of the "Dig For Victory" attitude of the war years, when people, even in towns, found places to lay down some carrots and turnips.

And health advice, although not as pervasive as today, extolled the virtues of greens — much to the disgust of many a schoolchild faced with limp boiled cabbage or bullet-hard sprouts.

Of course a square meal consisted of "meat and two veg", so there was no getting away from the humble vegetable.

There was also a problem that is rarely faced today, and that would astound youngsters. The insides of houses were so cold during an icy night night that veg stored in kitchen cupboards might freeze solid. Even after being thawed, veg that had suffered frosting had a strange taste.

Housewives, of course, had to find a way to defeat this.

May 28, 1950.
CUCUMBER — After peeling and slicing cucumber, lay the slices in a dish and give a good sprinkling of salt. Leave for an hour, then pour off all liquid before using for sandwiches or salad. Cucumber treated this way is more digestible. — **Miss A. Wilson, T.L.F. Grounds, Fulwell Road, Sunderland.**

January 21, 1951.
PUTS OOMPH INTO YOUR VEGETABLES — Stale or frost-bitten vegetables can be freshened up by soaking in very cold water to which a teaspoonful of bicarbonate of soda has been added. This should be done two or three hours before they're to be cooked. — **Mrs Johnston, 63 Port Dundas Road, Glasgow, wins a pair of towels.**

April 15, 1951.
ONIONS — Onions have a nasty habit of repeating after being eaten. This can be avoided by peeling and putting them for a few minutes in half a pint of boiling water to which ½ teaspoonful of bicarbonate of soda has been added. They can then be boiled or fried without being indigestible. — **Mrs V. Smith, Ploughlands, Maxton, Street, Boswells.**

July 8, 1951.
QUICK COOKING — Put butter beans in a vacuum flask of boiling water and leave overnight. Next day they are practically cooked, and just need heating up. — **Mrs M. Richardson, 2 Braughallan Gardens, Kirn.**

July 8, 1951.
FRYING TIP — Onions are more easily digested if fried this way. Fry for ten minutes in fat, then carefully add a half-cupful of boiling water, a little salt and let them simmer gently till cooked. — **Mrs Doris Shanley, c/o 245 Kilmarnock Road, Shawlands, Glasgow.**

July 15, 1951.
TASTY — Scrub new carrots and put them in a baking dish. Sprinkle over with brown sugar, chopped mint, and a few blobs of margarine. Cook until tender. The carrots retain their flavour. — **Mrs Murdoch, 67 New Dykes Road, Prestwick.**

July 29, 1951.
SALAD — Roll the smaller ingredients (such as chives, mint, parsley, &c.) firmly in a lettuce leaf and cut this roll with scissors. They are quickly and finely prepared for salad. — **Mrs A. G. Wright, 28 Berryhill Drive, Giffnock, Glasgow.**

August 19, 1951.
PARSLEY — Parsley can be kept fresh for days if it is put in a jam jar with no water. Make the jar airtight. Don't wash the parsley first. — **Mrs J. Stone, Jardine Terrace, Gartcosh.**

April 20, 1952.
TWO GOLDEN RULES FOR VEGETABLES — To get best results, vegetables that grown in the light (cabbage, &c.) should cook in the light — with lid off and put into boiling water. Those that grow in the dark (root vegetables) should cook in the dark — with lid on and put into cold water. — **Miss M. Ferbie, Burnside Cottage, Eaglesfield, by Lockerbie, wins a pair of towels.**

February 10, 1952.
ONION — A teaspoonful of grated onion put in a stew five minutes before serving is worth a whole onion put in earlier in the cooking. — **Mrs J. Brown, 12 Springfield Street, Leith.**

May 25, 1952.
FRESH VEG. — A piece of wet tissue paper folded and wrapped round vegetables such as cucumber will keep them fresh for days. — **Mrs Simpson, Wayside, St Andrews.**

July 6, 1952.
PEAS — When cooking garden peas, shell them and put them in a bowl with a nut of margarine and a lettuce leaf to cover peas. Place over boiling water until the peas are cooked. They're delicious when done this way — **Margaret Corbett, 30 Calder Street, Blantyre.**

August 3, 1952.
CAULIFLOWER — A squeeze of lemon into the boiling water will whiten cauliflower. — **Miss J. B. Cuthbert, 85 Comely Bank Avenue, Edinburgh.**

August 31, 1952.
PEAPODS — If peapods are limp, put them into cold water for an hour before using. Shell just before cooking and add a pinch of sugar to the water. — **Miss N. Gall, 1 Chapel Court, Justice Street, Aberdeen.**

March 23, 1952.
CARROTS — Cut carrots and turnips into small cubes, tie in muslin bags, and put into same pot with potatoes. They'll all be ready at the same time and easy to serve. — **Mrs W. Carmichael, 12 Longstone Av., Edinburgh, wins a pair of towels.**

March 30, 1952.
TOMATOES — Home-grown tomatoes will soon be in the shops again. My choice every time is the yellow variety. They're sweeter, have less acidity and more flesh than the red ones and they are better for you. — **J. McIntosh, Airdrie.**

March 30, 1952.
CRESS IN BOWLS — Mustard and cress can be grown quickly and easily in bulb bowls. Fill two bowls nearly to the top with fine earth. Sow mustard in one, cress in the other. You'll soon have a crop ready for salads. — **G. Hadden, 3 Neville Terrace, Priestgate, Peterboro'.**

December 7, 1952.
FROSTED VEG. — Prepare for cooking, then put them into a bowl of cold, salted water. (The water should cover them entirely.) Stand the bowl overnight in a warm room. The vegetables will then be ready for use. — **Miss D. MacGregor, Sutherland Cottage, Keir Street, Dunblane.**

March 8, 1953.
MEAT ROLL — When the mixture's in the jar, press into the centre a cleaned carrot. It adds flavour to the roll. — **Miss Wilson, Welfare Grounds, Fulwell Road, Sunderland.**

June 7, 1953.
LETTUCE — Don't chop lettuce with a knife — tear portions apart with fingers. This prevents the edges turning brown. — **Mrs I. Campbell, 29 Glenturret Street, Sandyhills, Glasgow.**

July 5, 1953.
ONIONS — Peel onions and place in saucepan with just enough water to cover them. Boil for three minutes. Then strain, slice and fry. I find they quickly become golden brown and don't burn. — **Mrs H. Smith, 14 John Street, Ruabon, Denbighshire.**

August 2, 1953.
FRESH CAULI — To keep cauliflower fresh, scoop out a cuplike hollow in the stalk and fill with water. Hang up cauliflower and it keeps fresh for several days. — **Miss S. McArthur, 24 Baldwin Avenue, Glasgow.**

November 22, 1953.
CARROTS — If winter carrots are put in boiling water for a few minutes they grate much easier. — **Mrs E. Paxton, Station Cottage, Heriot, Midlothian.**

December 20, 1953.
INDOOR PARSLEY — Fasten a piece of string to each side of a sponge to form a handle. Soak sponge in water twelve hours, then sprinkle with parsley seed. Hang by handle to hooks in a warm but airy place. Keep sponge moist. Result – a good crop of parsley. **— Mrs A. Easton, Nortonall, Melrose.**

May 16, 1954.
TOMATOES — When baking tomatoes whole, make a cut in the skin all round and they retain their shape. Apples don't break if done in the same way. — **Mrs J. Jamieson, Wamphray, by Moffat.**

May 16, 1954.
CELERY FOR SALADS — Celery tastes delicious if some cream cheese is spread inside the sticks before chopping into pieces. — **Mrs Williamson, 23 Saxon Road, Glasgow.**

December 5, 1954.
KEEPS FRESH — An unskinned onion cut in two and put inside a chicken which has been drawn, keeps it fresh for a considerable time. — **Miss F. Cole, 34 Stewart Street, Doncaster.**

April 24, 1955.
ONION — I find a clean, discarded nylon stocking good for storing onions. Sew a loop of tape at top of stocking and hang from a hook behind the larder door. — **Mrs J. Clifford, Strathview, Avonbridge, Falkirk, wins a pair of towels.**

May 1, 1955.
CABBAGE — If you've bought a spring cabbage which is rather limp, put the stalk into cold water, and it will turn crisp and fresh again. — **Mrs M. Ramsay, 40 Military Road, North Shields.**

June 19, 1955.
PARSLEY — Pick or buy a large bunch, spread out under grill and dry off very slowly until colour has turned. Store in air-tight tin or jar. When required, simply crumble with fingers over food. It's easier than chopping each time it's required. Mint can be done in the same way. — **Mrs J. Cochrane, Tighnaleigh, Smailes Lane, Rowlands Gill, County Durham.**

September 25, 1955.
CAULIFLOWERS — Boil cauliflowers with the stalk upwards to prevent scum discolouring the flower. – **Mrs A.C. Gow, c/o Major A.C. Gow, R.E., 229 D.C.R.E., B.A.O.R. 25.**

February 12, 1956.
SPROUTS — Before cooking brussels sprouts, make a cross cut in the end parts. This helps them to cook much quicker — and saves gas. — **Mrs E. Cochrane, 575 Crow Road, Jordanhill, Glasgow.**

February 26, 1956.
ONIONS — To keep onions whole when boiling, pack them into a wire frying basket. Place basket in boiling water, simmer till tender, then drain and serve. — **Mrs B. White, 70 Manuel Street, Goole.**

July 8, 1956.
CARROTS — Young carrots, which are small and difficult to hold, can be easily cleaned by sprinkling some common salt on a rather coarse, dry cloth and rubbing the carrots with this. They will be quite clean and free from skin. — **Mrs Slater, 17 Geddes Avenue, Portknockie.**

September 2, 1956.
PARSLEY — To store dried parsley for winter, I use a dark bottle to keep it in. I have found that by doing so the parsley never loses its colour. — **Mrs Johnston, 63 Port Dundas Road, Glasgow.**

September 2, 1956.
BEETROOT — Leave beetroot to cool in the water in which it is boiled. The skins come off clean without fear of cutting the flesh. — **Mrs M. Peebles, 6 Hill Crescent, Cupar.**

April 7, 1957.
ONIONS — After buying onions be sure to singe the roots. They will not sprout, and will keep fine and firm till required. — **Mrs M. Lancaster, 80 Niddrie Road, Glasgow.**

June 2, 1957.
PEAS — The best way to heat tinned peas is to tip them out into a colander. Wash and put into bowl. Sprinkle with a little sugar, cover with a lid, and steam. Done this way they taste like fresh peas. A sprig of mint can be added if desired. — **Mrs J. R. Black, 4 New Block, Cruden Bay.**

June 16, 1957.
ONIONS — To prevent onions from separating while slicing, cut off the tops, but leave on the roots. — **Mrs Davidson, 16 Woodlands Crescent, Turriff.**

December 29, 1957.
FOR FLAVOURING — Don't throw away a sprouting onion. Set it in a shallow dish filled with soil and keep damp. It sends up plenty of green shoots which can be used to flavour soup and stews. — **Miss Boyle, Dunacree, Aberfeldy.**

June 1, 1958.
TRY IT — Mint is growing well just now. I chop it up with a little sugar added and dissolve a greengage jelly with vinegar. Use only part of the jelly at a time, according to the amount of mint. It keeps well and there's no flavour lost. — **H. Brotherhood, 65 Comiston Road, Newton Estate, Lancaster.**

February 15, 1959.
TOMATOES — When baking stuffed tomatoes, try putting them into greased patty tins. This keeps them a nice shape and they are attractive to take to the table. — **M. Symington, 7 Fereneze Crescent, Glasgow.**

March 15, 1959.
ONIONS — After peeling or cooking onions, use a little deodorant on the palms of the hands and touch under the nails with an orange stick. All traces of odour vanish. — **Miss I. C. Mackay, Arch House, Lairg.**

March 29, 1959.
ONION FLAVOURING — Many families, while appreciating the flavour of onion, do not like the vegetable itself. This can be overcome by using a small portion of onion soup as a thickening and flavouring agent. A shilling packet is sufficient for a number of stews. — **Mrs Marie T. Patterson, Cairndhu, 44 Oak Street, Windermere.**

April 19, 1959.
CELERY SALT — Place celery leaves in a warm oven to dry out until crisp. Then crush to a powder and mix with an equal amount of salt. Bottle and use as required. — **Mrs B. Anderson, c/o 4 Knox Place, Tillydrone, Aberdeen.**

April 19, 1959.
PARSLEY — If your parsley has all shrivelled up with the hard frost, stand it in a bowl of boiling water for a few hours. The result will be nice, fresh, green parsley. — **Mrs Paterson, Wester Parkgate, Parkgate, Dumfries.**

June 21, 1959.
CUCUMBER — To keep cucumber fresh, immerse in dish of cold water until required for salad. — **Mrs R. W. Wilson, 33 Heugh Street, Falkirk.**

July 19, 1959.
GREEN PEAS — The best way to cook green peas is to put a few lettuce leaves in the pan under the peas, add a piece of butter and put the lid on tightly. Cook slowly for 10 minutes, without water. — **Miss W. Martin, 34 Balgarvie Crescent, Cupar.**

September 20, 1959.
PARSLEY — Parsley can be kept fresh all through winter by picking it fresh and dry from the garden. Remove stalks and put alternate layers of parsley and cooking salt in a large jar until it is filled to the top. Keep tightly closed and use as required. — **Mrs F. W. Hamilton, King's Arms Hotel, Maybole.**

September 27, 1959.
BEANS — Use scissors when cutting kidney beans. I find this much quicker than a knife and the beans are more evenly shaped. — **Mrs L. Mason, 18 Garfourth Road, Liverpool.**

1950s Pamphlet — Do you make the very best use of vegetables when they are plentiful? Doctors and food experts all urge us to eat more of this sort of fare, and since this is so, you see how important it is for you to think of ways to include more vegetables in your family's diet. Of course, if your idea of cooked vegetables is watery boiled cabbage or turnip you will probably have difficulty in getting the children to touch them. But when they have tasted cauliflower smothered in cheese sauce, cabbage filled with a tasty meat stuffing, or green peas as an accompaniment to poached eggs, you will find there is nothing they like better. Here are some recipes which should help you.

CARROT MOULD

3 Large Carrots
1 Egg
1 oz. Butter
Salt, Pepper
1 tablespoonful Chopped Parsley

You don't need meat when you serve this dish, and you need not be a vegetarian to enjoy it.

First thing to do is to well wash and scrape the carrots, then boil for two hours.

When cooked drain and rub through a sieve. Melt the butter and add to the carrots, heating them thoroughly. Beat the egg and add it with salt and pepper.

Grease a mould and pour in the mixture and press well down. Place in the oven for 10 minutes, turn on to a hot dish and sprinkle on top the parsley and serve with melted butter.

BAKED CABBAGE

2 tablespoonfuls Chopped Cooked Bacon
1 Firm Cabbage
2 Eggs
2 tablespoonfuls Butter
3 tablespoonfuls Milk
Salt and Pepper

Making the Most of Vegetables

Saving Time With Chips

Cabbage cooked this way is another delicious dish which you should try.

Boil the cabbage in the usual way. When tender, drain, chop it finely, add the butter, the beaten eggs, milk and bacon. Season and mix all carefully. Turn the mixture into a pie-dish and bake until it is browned on the top. Scraps of butter dotted over the top hasten the browning operation.

BAKED CABBAGE

Any Cooked Vegetables
1 cup Milk
2 cups Flour
2 Eggs,
2 tablespoonfuls Cheese

It is remarkable how well vegetables can rise to the occasion when the meat fails to arrive.

For this dish almost any vegetable can be used, either left over or freshly cooked. Make a batter with milk, flour, and the beaten yolks of the eggs. Beat the whites of the eggs until stiff, and grate the cheese. Stir these ingredients into batter until all is smooth. Now slice the chosen vegetables, which must be cooked already, and dip each slice into the batter. Then fry in deep fat until brown.

TOMATOES AU GRATIN

4 to 6 tomatoes, 2 oz. Grated Cheese, Pepper and Salt.

This is one of the nicest ways to serve tomatoes.

Scald the tomatoes in boiling water and remove the skin. Leave whole or cut in slices. Lay in a fire-proof dish. Season with pepper and salt and cover with the grated cheese. Put into a hot oven for about 10 minutes till brown on the top.

Chapter 15

Top Tips For Tatties

THE humble tattie. This native of Peru and Bolivia was, it is often said, first brought to these shores by Sir Francis Drake. This isn't actually true, it was introduced by Spanish traders at least a decade before Drake's triumphant tattie "tada" of 1586. But what is indisputably a fact is that tatties grow well in our moist, loamy farmland . . . and we love them.

There are traditionally three main ways to cook a potato. Boiled, roasted or fried as chips.

There are rumours that some people bake potatoes in the oven, but this would take an awful lot of gas, quickly depleting the meter, and is therefore frowned upon — unless the person doing the potato baking is affy pan loafy.

It is traditional to mash them, with a little butter and milk, when coupling the tuber with a portion of chopped-up and boiled steak beef to make the greatest and most celebrated achievement in mankind's culinary history — mince and tatties.

June 22, 1952.
POTATOES — To preserve the flavour of new potatoes, cover them with damp earth, either in a box or in the garden, till required. — **Mrs Wm. Gibson, Mark Holm, Victoria Place, Stranraer.**

July 20, 1952.
TIP FOR TATTIES — Here's one way of having new potatoes for Christmas dinner. Use a tin drum to hold two stone of Epicures. Fill the bottom with three inches of dry sawdust, then pack in potatoes up to three inches from the top of the drum. Fill with dry sawdust, pack tightly, and make airtight. — **T. Williams, Craigend Hostel, Kilmun.**

May 6, 1951.
POTATO TIP — When peeling potatoes, do so with a wire mesh pot cleaner. This saves waste, is easier on the hands, and preserves the layer next to the skin, which has a high food value. — **T. Macaulay, 38 The Wynd, Cumbernauld.**

February 18, 1951.
BAKED POTATOES — Allow the potatoes to lie in hot water for 15 minutes before baking. This improves the flavour and saves fuel by reducing cooking time. If crisp, brown potatoes are desired, brush over with dripping before putting in the oven. — **Mrs J. May, New House, Huntingtower, by Perth.**

July 15, 1951.
POTATOES — A speedy way of skinning new potatoes is to soak them in cold water for five minutes, then rub briskly with a piece of coarse curtain net. The skin falls away easily. — **Miss N. McGrail, 115 Roslea Drive, Glasgow E.1.**

September 2, 1951.
KEEP COLOUR — If potatoes are peeled and left overnight, a little milk added to the water in which they're kept will save them going brown. — **Mrs J. Napier, 14 Dalgety Street, Edinburgh.**

June 3, 1951.
NEW POTATOES — When boiling new potatoes, boil first without salt, drain and put in fresh boiling water. This takes away the "green" taste new potatoes quite often have. — **Mrs H. Tocher, 61 West Church Street, Buckie.**

June 10, 1951.
POTATOES — When baking potatoes in their jackets, always prick each one with a fork immediately it is removed from the oven. This allows the steam to escape. There is no chance of the potatoes being soggy. — **Mrs Barbara Macmillan, 23 Droverhall Place, Crossgates.**

March 11, 1951.
HANDY POTATO — Keep a small potato handy when cutting up onions. Run the knife blade through, and all smell vanishes. Also rub the potato on the fingers. — **Mrs M. Thayne, 334 Nuneaton Street, Glasgow.**

March 9, 1952.
POTATOES — When your potatoes are over-boiled and a bit mushy, lay a thick cloth over a colander and empty them into it. Gather up the cloth and squeeze out all the water. A light, fluffy ball of potatoes remains. — **Mrs K. Ferriday, Annfield, Kingskettle.**

January 13, 1952.
FROSTED — To take away the sweet frosted taste which is so unpleasant in potatoes, first bring them to the boil, and boil for five minutes. Then add one cupful of cold water and quarter teaspoonful salt. Boil in the usual way until cooked, and the potatoes will be as fresh as from the garden. For a larger quantity, just add more water. — **C. Riddell, c/o 257 Croftfoot Road, Glasgow.**

May 24, 1953.
NEW POTATOES — To lighten task of scraping new potatoes — and save hands being stained — first stand potatoes in basin of boiling water for a few minutes. Skins will slip off. — **Miss B. Fraser, Millbank, Port Elphinstone, Inverurie.**

October 4, 1953.
BOILED IN JACKETS — Before boiling potatoes in their jackets, cut off a thin strip of skin right round the centre of each. After being boiled, the remaining skin will slip off easily. This prevents waste of the best part of the potato, which is next to the skin. — **Mrs M. Thompson, 12 Davidson Street, Lancaster.**

February 28, 1954.
QUICKLY COOKED — When you need roast potatoes in a hurry, peel them and cut as for roasting. Then do them for 15 minutes in the chip pan. — **Mrs Turner, 145 Harrington Road, London.**

June 19, 1955.
POTATOES — Don't send potatoes to the table in a covered dish. They absorb their own moisture and become sodden. — **Mrs D. K. Tolley, 111 Cricklade Street, Cirencester.**

November 13, 1955.
BAKED POTATOES — When baking potatoes put them on a wire pastry tray. The tray, being raised on small feet, allows the heat to circulate evenly and the potatoes need no turning. — **Mrs Lockhart, Clifton Cottage, Kirk Yetholm, Kelso.**

January 22, 1956.
QUICK COOKING — If you remove the centre from potatoes with an apple corer they bake or roast in half the time. — **Mrs E. Muers, 19 Cecil Street, Sunderland.**

February 19, 1956.
PIQUANT FLAVOUR — A little mayonnaise or salad cream added to mashed potatoes gives them an extra flavour and takes away any earthy taste in old potatoes. — **Mrs M. Miller, 18 Fordyce Street, Glasgow.**

June 10, 1956.
GOOD SLICER — I find a wire egg-slicer a boon for neatly slicing new potatoes for salads, &c. — **Miss M. Williams, 17 Wrenbury Street, Holt Road, Edge-Hill, Lancs.**

August 26, 1956.
POTATOES — When frying new potatoes, dip each slice in fine oatmeal. This makes them lovely and brown, and adds to the flavour. — **Miss E. C. Coney, Dunara, Ardrishaig.**

June 30, 1957.
POTATOES — If potatoes are overcooked to pulp, and you cannot drain all water off, mix in some dry breadcrumbs with usual seasoning. Add butter, and mash all together. The crumbs absorb the water, and are not noticed. The result is nice, fluffy potatoes. — **Mrs D. Irvine, 30 Learmonth Grove, Edinburgh.**

September 29, 1957.
POTATOES — Before baking potatoes in their skins, grease the skins first to keep them tender. This also improves the flavour and cuts down on cooking time. — **Miss C. J. Harvey, 20 Southside Road, Inverness.**

October 20, 1957.
ROAST POTATOES — Roast potatoes are especially nice if you scratch the surface of each potato with a fork after they have been part boiled. Place in the roast fat after lightly dusting with fine salt. This makes them crisp and more attractive. Keep turning occasionally until they are a golden brown, and serve very hot. — **Mrs Scott, Benholm, Montrose.**

November 3, 1957.
BAKING POTATOES — Use a patty tin instead of a baking dish when baking potatoes in their jackets. Put one in each section. They're then easily removed from the oven. — **Mrs J. Cunningham, Park View, Blackford.**

December 7, 1958.
POTATO PEELER — If your peeler chokes up, insert a screwdriver under the cutting edge and open up slightly. Rub carborundum stone along cutting edge to sharpen. — **Mrs R. C. Marnie, Sunbury, 12 Aubery Crescent, Largs.**

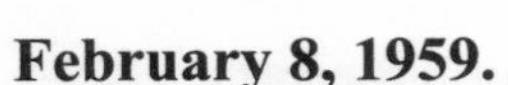

February 8, 1959.
DISCOLOURED POTATOES — When potatoes are old and get black while cooking, add half a teaspoonful of baking soda to the water 15 minutes before dishing. You will be surprised how white they become. — **M. Taylor, Elleslea, South Whitehills, Forfar.**

February 15, 1959.
CRISPER CHIPS — When chips are being made, frosted potatoes are apt to turn brown before the inside is cooked. Try pouring boiling water over them, let them stand for a few minutes, drain, then pop them into the boiling fat. — **Mrs E. Robertson, Enfield Place, 26 Manse Street, Crossgates, Cowdenbeath.**

July 5, 1959.
QUICKER — To clean new potatoes quickly, soak them in hot water to which a little salt has been added. After a short time, rub with a nylon pot scrubber. The skins will come off easily and don't stain the hands. — **Mrs L. Morton, 12 Hillfoot Terrace, Carluke.**

July 19, 1959.
NEW WAY WITH POTATOES — Roll freshly-boiled potatoes in melted butter, then grated cheese. Place in a single layer in a shallow baking dish and put under the grill until the cheese melts and browns. — **Mrs W. Stewart, 51 Cairndhuna Terrace, Wick.**

September 20, 1959.
POTATOES — To boil potatoes that you intend to go to mash, first put on in cold water and part boil with salt as usual. Then strain and put back on cooker and do in their own steam, with only a peep of gas. — **Mrs Cable, 45 Fraser Avenue, Wardie, Edinburgh.**

October 4, 1959.
BETTER POTATOES — Some potatoes just now are very soft and break up easily when cooking. To prevent this, add one tablespoonful of vinegar to the water before boiling. Boil 15 minutes, strain, but leave a little liquid at bottom of pan. Turn gas low and steam until potatoes are dry. — **Mrs A. Macnamara, 1 Ferry Road Avenue, Edinburgh.**

November 22, 1959.
POTATO CHANGE — For a change the other day, I added a fourpenny portion of cheese and onion spread to mashed potatoes instead of butter. We all enjoyed it very much. — **Mrs Eileen G. Leiper, 153 Victoria Road, Torry, Aberdeen.**

Let 'em sneeze...

I've had hot Bovril!

Crowded buses are full of coughs and sneezes. So are railway carriages, Tubes and subways too. So, before you travel, make sure you help yourself to real resistance against catching 'flu or a cold from your companions by downing a good hot cup of Bovril.

Doctors know the value of Bovril. One writes: "For over 30 years I have prescribed Bovril. Particularly do I find it useful to patients during the cold weather." There's nothing like Bovril for keeping you fit and well. Into Bovril goes the concentrated goodness of prime lean beef. Bovril also helps supply you with those important B vitamins, Riboflavin and Niacin. Each cup of Bovril you drink gives you, in fact, *as much as one-fifth of your total daily need!*

No doubt about it. Drinking Bovril helps to keep you well. What a delicious drink it is too.

BOVRIL

keeps you warm– keeps you well

Chapter 16

Before Fridges

Even by 1959, only 13% of UK homes boasted refrigerators — and they were all the posh folk. Indeed, there were very few "mod cons" of any description. Kitchen tasks were done by hand.

But while other problems could be solved by elbow grease and a willing attitude, there wasn't any way to stop nature taking its course. It is an inescapable fact that, if stored at room temperature, some types of food will quickly go off.

So keeping foodstuffs fresh wasn't easy, and became especially difficult in the summer months.

But clever people found clever ways…

May 21, 1950.
FRESH — to keep butter firm in hot weather, fill a box with wet sand, leaving a space to place the dish containing butter. Add water to sand when it gets too dry. — **Miss J. Harle, 14 Rectory Road, Hetton-le-Hole, Durham, wins this week's guinea.**

October 1, 1950.
LEMONS — To keep lemons fresh and juicy, keep them in a cool place in a bowl of cold water, changing the water each day. Leave plenty of room for lemons to float in the bowl. — **Mrs Fraser, Sunfield, Inchmaris, Banchory.**

August 13, 1950.
FRESH MEAT — To freshen meat in hot weather wash it thoroughly in salt water, then dry it. Rub all over with dry mustard to which has been added a little salt. — **Miss Margaret McGregor, Sutherland Cottage, Keir Street, Dunblane.**

November 5, 1950.
LEMONS — Lemons will keep if a candle is melted and the wax smeared over the fruit. Allow to cool, and store in a cold place. When ready to use, crack the wax and it will peel off easily. — **Mrs C. Dolan, 43 Mansion Street, Possilpark, Glasgow.**

May 27, 1951.
To Keep Butter From Running On Hot Days — Clean a large flower pot and plug the hole with a cork, so that the narrow end of the cork is inside. Tap cork on the outside with a small hammer until it is level with the bottom of the pot. This makes the pot leak-proof. Place the pot in a vessel of cold water and it acts as a first-class butter cooler. — **Mrs R. Hill, 12 Bryson Street, Grahamston, Falkirk, wins a pair of towels.**

November 1, 1953.
CHEESE— I find that by wrapping my cheese ration in waxed paper it keeps fresh longer and doesn't go dry. — **Mrs M. Lindsay, 42 Croft Road, Cambuslang, Glasgow.**

April 25, 1954.
BANANAS — To prevent bananas turning black and soft, store in a pan with a tight fitting lid. — **Mrs R. Parnaby, 41 Howard Street, North Shields.**

September 4, 1955.
FRESH MILK — I empty milk into a vacuum flask the minute I get it. Next morning it's as fresh as when it arrived, no matter how hot the weather. — **J. Boyd, 6 Pattison Street, Dalmuir.**

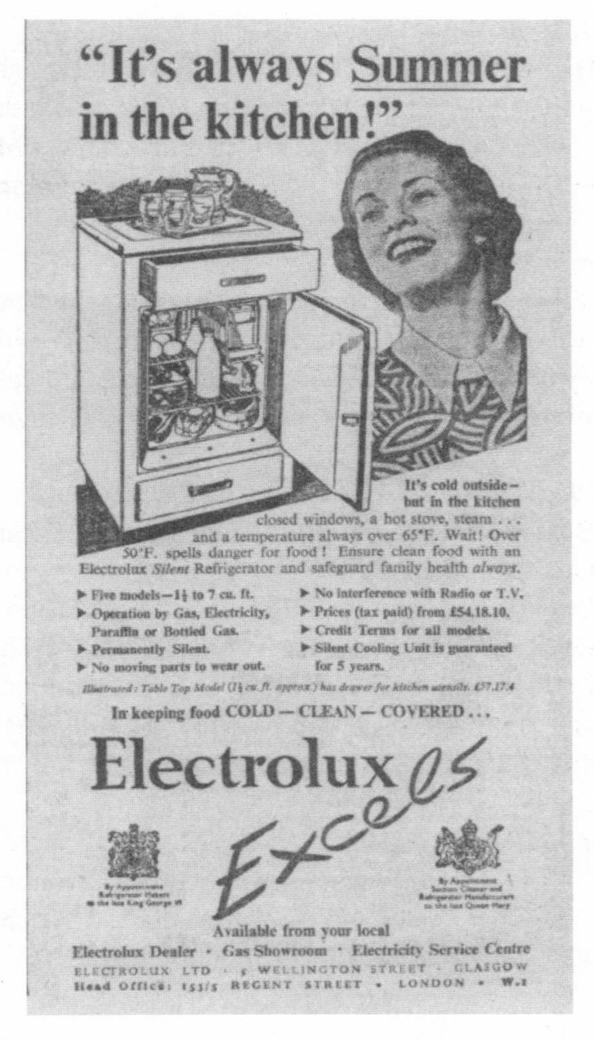

July 29, 1956.
TOMATOES — When tomatoes get soft, put them into a bowl of cold water in which a teaspoonful of salt has been dissolved. Leave for an hour, and they are firm again. — **Mrs A. Morrison, The Cottage, New Blyth, by Turriff.**

August 18, 1957.
PARSLEY — Placed in a pan with the lid on, parsley keeps for long enough. — **Jean H. Young, Queen's House, Kelso.**

Chapter 17

We Hae Meat

As the Selkirk Grace says: "Some hae meat and canna eat, And some wad eat that want it, But we hae meat and we can eat, Sae let the Lord be Thankit!"

But, sometimes, we didn't have meat. Or what we did have was stringy and of low quality.

Meat and bacon were the last food items to come off rationing. It wasn't until the summer of 1954, more than 14 long years after rationing began, that people could get as much meat as they could afford to buy.

Even when you did have coupons for meat — and your chosen butcher had stock — you could never quite be sure what it would be. It might be mutton, ham, pork, bacon, or, if you were very lucky that week, good quality British beef.

After 1954, of course, everyone got a little more adventurous.

Creative dishes such as beef olives began to be talked about. And a pork joint rubbed with ginger. Then we went all "continental" and put slices of pineapple on gammon.

Those were decadent days indeed.

This chapter is also unique, I feel justified to say. It is the only place in the modern world where readers can find information on how best to parcel up poultry to send to a friend or relative using the Royal Mail postal service.

May 28, 1950.
RABBITS — Do not soak a rabbit in salt water. This tends to harden the meat. Use a teaspoonful of bicarbonate of soda in the water and leave the rabbit in it for an hour. Rinse well. This cleans and takes away the strong flavour, and even the toughest rabbit cooks tenderly.
— R. Daly, 30 Manse Street, Saltcoats.

August 27, 1950.
RAW MEAT — Never allow raw meat to lie in its own juice. Place on a wire privet, or prop up with a spoon to permit air to circulate round it. — **Mrs M. Thayne, 334 Nuneaton Street, Glasgow.**

September 17, 1950.
ROASTING TIP — When roasting a joint, tie some fat in a muslin bag and hang it from the top grid of the oven. The fat will melt and drip over the joint, basting it beautifully without any need of attention. If you add some salt and pepper and any other flavouring you like, it gives the joint a good rich flavour.
— Mrs J. A. Douglas, 53 Clouston Street, Glasgow.

January 21, 1951.
RABBIT — Next time you stew a rabbit, pop a handful of prunes into the pot. They flavour and colour the gravy. The two go surprisingly well together. — **Mrs V. Harrison, Dundee.**

August 19, 1951.
DOUGHBALLS — Lay a piece of greaseproof paper on top of the stew or mince and place doughballs on the paper. They don't absorb the gravy and are light and fluffy. — **Mrs McCook, 260 Bearsden Road, Glasgow.**

December 16, 1951.
MAKES TENDER — If you're cooking a chicken which looks as if it might be tough, place two or three peeled potatoes inside the bird. These will cook as the bird cooks, and the steam from them will help to make the bird tender. — **Miss W. Farquharson, Brackla, Nairn.**

September 30, 1951.
FOWLS BY POST — When sending a fowl by post, clean and then place an onion inside the fowl. It will arrive in perfect condition. — **Mrs A. Henderson, Smithy House, Bilbster, Wick.**

June 10, 1951.
SAUSAGES — When skinning sausages, hold each one for a second or two under the running tap. The skin will come off easily and cleanly. — **Mrs C. H. Stewart, 19 Broomlea Crescent, Edinburgh 12.**

June 17, 1951.
COOKING A FOWL — When boiling a fowl, wrap it in greaseproof paper and tie securely before putting into the boiling water. This method keeps the fowl moist and is also a great benefit when lifting it out of the pot. — **Mrs W. Peebles, Wilmar, Dairsie, Cupar, Fife.**

July 8, 1951.
KEEPS MEAT FRESH IN HOT WEATHER — Here's a foolproof method of keeping meat fresh in summer. Dissolve 1 oz. salt and 1 oz. sugar in a pint of vinegar, and boil. When the mixture's cold, brush it over meat, then put meat in a cool place. Rinse meat under the cold tap before using, and use less salt in cooking. The mixture will keep indefinitely in a corked bottle, and this quantity should be enough to treat meat for several weeks. — **Mrs L. McRae, 53 Copland Road, Glasgow S.W.1, wins a pair of towels.**

September 21, 1952.
TOPICAL TIP — In Belgium I tasted steak sausage and steak patties with stewed apples; steak and kidney with prunes. But best of all was — two pieces of toast (unbuttered) with two slices Kraft cheese (heated to melting stage) and topped with a large slice of lean, boiled ham. — **E. H., Edinburgh.**

October 12, 1952.
BOILED HAM — When boiling ham at home, add the juice of half a lemon to the water. This keeps the flesh pink and the fat white. — **Mrs E. Annal, 46a Moodie Street, Dunfermline.**

October 12, 1952.

PERFECT DISH FOR WINTER

LAST Sunday The Doc wrote that a plate of "stovies" and a glass of milk make a perfect winter meal. He explained that the onions in "stovies" stimulate the cells of the lungs and bronchial tubes and keep them fighting fit. So now many readers have written asking how to make "stovies". One reader, Mrs Bastiman, of 3 Midhurst Road, Thorntree Estate, Middlesbrough, says: "Since coming south of the Border, I've never tasted them or come across anyone who could make them."

Righto, Mrs Bastiman and the rest who wrote — here's the recipe:- Ingredients — 2 lb. potatoes, 2 onions, 1 oz. dripping, ½ pint hot water or gravy, seasoning. Melt fat and fry previously-sliced onions. Prepare and slice potatoes and put into pan. Add hot water or gravy and the seasoning. Simmer slowly until ready, stirring occasionally to prevent burning.

June 1, 1952.
TOO SALTY — A lump of sugar will take away the over-salted taste from savoury dishes without leaving any taste of sugar. — **Miss A. Kennedy, Daisy Bank, Braemar.**

FOOD NEWS **November 16, 1952.**

CANNED MEAT PILING UP IN WAREHOUSES
– BY OUR FOOD REPORTER

THERE'S a glut of tinned meats, including Irish stew, luncheon meat, minced beef loaf, and Polish chopped pork. They are piling up in warehouses.

In an effort to clear stocks, some are being cut in price.

Small supplies of shelled peanuts — the first for several years — are expected in the shops for Christmas. Some are likely to be sold in sixpenny packets, and perhaps salted.

Tinned vegetables, especially carrots and celery, will be more plentiful this winter.

Because of the rice shortage, Kellogg's have had to cut the allocation of Rice Crispies to shops by about 75 per cent.

March 9, 1952.
RABBIT — Rabbit whitens better if soaked overnight in water with two large tablespoonfuls of vinegar added instead of salt. This applies particularly now, when the season for rabbits is nearly over. — **J. A. Muir, 7 Chesser Grove, Edinburgh.**

January 27, 1952.
TAKES THE TOUGHNESS OUT OF MEAT — To improve a tough-looking joint of meat, make cuts through it from top to bottom with a sharp knife. Insert thin pieces of lard dipped in salt and pepper. Meat is usually roasted this way in Sweden. — **Miss Christina E. Robertson, 5 Stanley Place, Edinburgh, wins a pair of towels.**

FOOD NEWS January 18, 1953.
THIS week's meat ration will comprise about half home-killed beef. The remainder is in mutton (mostly home).

But you may get a bit Canterbury lamb, frozen mutton, pork, or even Patagonian lamb.

FOOD NEWS January 25, 1953.

PORK – OFF RATION BY EASTER

– BY OUR FOOD REPORTER

PORK is expected to come off the ration before Easter. Although the bacon ration is reduced from today (five to four oz.), it's likely to be restored in about a month.

De-control of price and quality of sausages is being considered. De-control would mean better quality and wider choice. Prices are not expected to rise.

There'll be a good percentage of beef in your increased meat ration. In some areas it'll be roughly fifty-fifty beef and mutton. But Glasgow folk will get only 25 per cent. beef.

Butchers believe an all-the-year-round ration of 2s worth is being aimed at — possibly reached in penny stages. They feel this level can be maintained if we get all the meat Argentina has promised us.

Last year, when the ration was up to 2s 2d worth, many housewives didn't take it all.

FOOD NEWS March 1, 1953.

THERE'S better news about this week's meat ration. About half will be in beef.

But the mutton part is just as over-fat, and butchers expect to be left with some of it.

Last week, one Glasgow butcher cancelled 120 lb. of his coming allocation — and he hadn't put a knife in his previous week's supply! Another butcher cancelled 150 lb. The buyer for a string of multiple shops didn't take hundreds of pounds.

Butchers in Scotland have several hundred tons of surplus fat cut from over-fat mutton and beef and pork.

Part of the margarine ration is to be issued in bulk form instead of pre-packed. This has been necessary because of flood damage to one of the largest factories in the south.

But the proportion of this bulk marge isn't likely to exceed 20 per cent. of the ration.

November 8, 1953.

ROASTING — When roasting meat or fowl, I find it best to cover it with several thicknesses of cheese-cloth and baste over it. Done this way, it comes from the oven juicy and tender. — **Mrs A. Southwell, Hythe, Alberta, Canada.**

October 17, 1954.

BRISKET — Leave brisket or rolled mutton in stock in which it has been cooked until ready to serve. It retains the natural juices. — **Mrs A. Wallace, 6 Clepington Street, Dundee.**

November 7, 1954.

TOO SALTY — If the breakfast ham is salty, put the ham to be fried in a soup plate, pour a little milk over it, and let it stand half an hour. — **Mrs McKendrick, 64 Bridgend Avenue, Port Glasgow.**

November 28, 1954.
OX TONGUE — After boiling ox tongue, twist into shape while warm to fit a round cake tin with loose bottom. When the tongue has set it's easily removed by pressing the bottom of the tin.
— Mrs Gibson, 112 Silverknowes Road, Edinburgh.

April 10, 1955.
TOUGH FOWL — Instead of stuffing in the usual way, fill with raw potatoes. Cook slowly in a covered dish. Steam from the potatoes makes the flesh of the fowl as tender as spring chicken.
— Mrs Mary Boswell, 12 Peter Street, Workington.

January 22, 1956.
ROAST CHICKEN — Make a dough of plain flour and water, roll out thinly. Grease chicken with fat, put in roasting tin, and cover with rolled-out dough. Roast in the usual manner. When cooked, lift off dough, which has baked into a hard crust — leaving the flesh of the fowl white and tender. **— Mrs Kay, Dellwood, 102 Comely Place, Falkirk.**

March 4, 1956.
TIME SAVER — When making beef olives, it is a good plan to secure with wooden cocktail sticks. They are easier than thread to remove before serving. **— Mrs G. W. Mackay, 21 Queen's Gate, Dowanhill, Glasgow.**

April 15, 1956.
ROASTING — When roasting, turn the oven gas out 15 minutes before the meat is ready to come out. The heat of the oven will finish the cooking. **— Miss A. Wilson, Recreation Grounds, Fulwell Road, Sunderland.**

June 3, 1956.
SAUSAGES — Fry sausages without separating them. Fried in a string they have more room to expand when hot. This prevents them bursting out of their skins. — **M. Whiteside, 83 Aitkenhead Avenue, Coatbridge.**

June 10, 1956.
GRILLING — When grilling bacon, I find using kitchen scissors a much easier way of turning the rashers. — **Mrs J. Grieve, 48 Lady Helen Street, Kirkcaldy.**

July 8, 1956.
EASY TO HANDLE — When boiling a piece of ham or beef, I put it into a muslin bag. This makes it so easy to lift out. — **Mrs M. Stout, Holmside, 105 Kells Lane, Low Fell, Gateshead.**

August 26, 1956.
SALTY BACON — If you have salty bacon, lay it on a dinner plate and pour boiling water from the kettle over it. Drain before frying. — **Mrs I. Imrie, Braehead, Oakley, Dunfermline.**

December 2, 1956.
NEW FLAVOUR ROAST — Have you tried ginger with roast pork? Rub the roast with salt, pepper and a little ginger. During roasting sprinkle with a tablespoonful of brown sugar. Your roast will have a new flavour. — **Mrs H. Sadler, Fair Acre, Lothersdale, Keighley.**

April 14, 1957.
GRAVY — I've found the best and most appetising way of thickening gravy for stews, roasts, &c., is to grate a small potato into it 15 minutes before serving, and simmer rather quickly. This does not give the glossy floury effect when cornflour or plain flour is used. — **Mrs Helen M. Galloway, 26 Alexandra Street, Kirkcaldy.**

August 18, 1957.
SUPPER SAVOURY — Next time you are having sausages for supper, cut a slit down the side of each and insert a small piece of cheese. Grill in the usual way. You will find them delicious. — **Mrs G. Elrick, 627 Holburn Street, Aberdeen.**

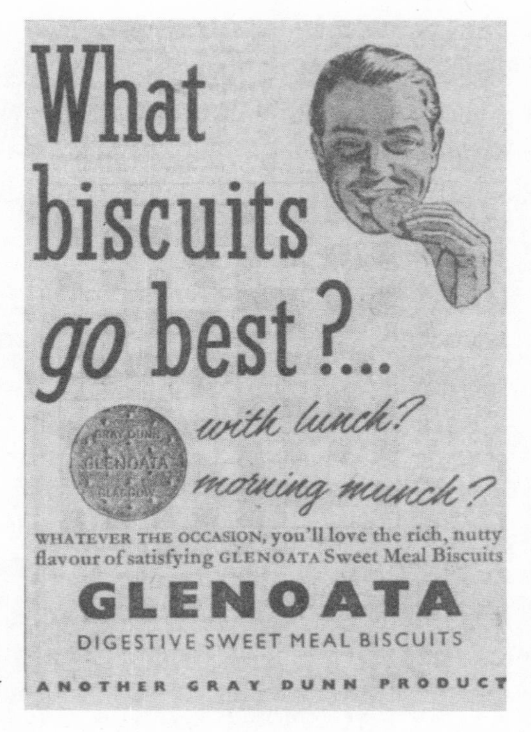

January 26, 1958.
RICHER GRAVY — When roasting meat put a small dish of flour into the oven, alongside. The flour browns slowly, and is ready to mix into a rich, brown gravy when the meat is done. — **Mrs A. Tocher, 61 West Church Street, Buckie.**

July 20, 1958.
MEAT PASTE — Meat paste which has been opened keeps longer if sealed with a teaspoonful of melted butter. Pour over the top and allow to set. — **Mrs Catherine Wilson, 22 Ferguslie Walk, Paisley.**

April 13, 1958.
GOOD MIXER — If you don't possess a mix-all, a good substitute for mixing gravies and sauces is an ordinary screw top jar. Put in the ingredients and shake well. All lumps are then removed. — **Mrs Morton, Rochefort, 8 Well House Drive, Leeds.**

August 24, 1958.
STEAK MINCE — Before putting steak through the mincer, give it a short beating with the blunt edge of a heavy kitchen knife. The steak goes through so much easier and quicker with no clogging of the holes of the mincer. — **Mrs J. Fullarton, 5 Cambuslea Road, Ayr.**

November 30, 1958.
TINNED MEAT — Run hot water over a tin of meat before opening it. This melts the jelly and the meat slides out easily. — **Mrs E. Blake, 46 Seamore Street, Glasgow, wins a pair of towels.**

January 11, 1959.
PRESSED TONGUE — If a proper dish is not available for pressing tongue after boiling, use a long length of butter muslin (or other fine cloth) and bind it tightly round the tongue and secure. Place between plates with a heavy weight on top and leave overnight. — **Miss S. Harrow, 29 Bank Street, Greenock.**

February 22, 1959.
FLAVOUR — If 1 teacupful vinegar and 6 or 8 cloves are added to each gallon of water when boiling ham, the flavour is greatly improved. Let the ham cool in the water in which it has been boiled You will find it is then deliciously moist. — **A. Carr, Henhill Farm, Chathill, Northumberland.**

May 10, 1959.
KETCHUP FLAVOURING — When using ketchup to flavour stews or other dishes, be sparing with the salt as the ketchup itself imparts a salty flavour. — **Mrs B. Finnie, 12 Mearns Street, Aberdeen.**

May 31, 1959.
JUICY JOINT — If your Sunday joint is lean, you won't find it dry next day if you pour the gravy over and leave overnight. — **Miss L. Rowell, 94 Front Street, Newbiggin by Sea.**

June 21, 1959.
MEAT IN HOT WEATHER — Pour a little vinegar into a large dish and place two pieces of stick across the dish. Stand the meat on the sticks. The vinegar wards off flies and also helps to keep the meat sweet. — **Mrs Ellis, 121 Sinclair Drive, Glasgow.**

July 5, 1959.
DELICIOUS CHOPS — To give chops that "different flavour" squeeze some lemon juice on them before grilling. — **Mrs M. MacDonald, Moy Farm, Tulloch, R.S.O., Inverness-shire.**

July 19, 1959.
FRESH MEAT — When you take meat home from the butcher's, hang it up or place it on a wire cake or grill tray. The juices drip away freely. If the meat is put on a plate, the juices collect round the bottom of the joint, where they go stale and give the meat a tainted taste. — **Mrs Margaret John, 35 Coed Saeson Crescent, Sketty, Swansea.**

October 11, 1959.
MEAT JOINT — Before putting a joint or cold meat in a fridge, wrap it in waxed paper. This keeps the meat from becoming dry and discoloured. — **Mrs E. Moore, 74 Gipton Wood Road, Leeds.**

October 18, 1959.
TASTY — Having had sliced pineapple served with ham in a restaurant and enjoyed it, I tried smoked bacon with tinned pears lightly fried and found it delicious. — **Mrs M. L. Cameron, 16 Falmouth Avenue, Flixton, nr. Manchester.**

November 1, 1959.
BACON — Bacon will keep longer if you separate the rashers and put them between clean greaseproof paper, so that they are not in direct contact. — **Miss M. Grieve, 51 Albert Place, Galashiels.**

November 8, 1959.
DUCK — When plucking a duck, remove large feathers by hand and rub off down with a soft pencil rubber. These can be removed in a few minutes. — **Mrs V. Pirie, 60 King Street, Nairn.**

November 15, 1959.
APPLE SAUCE — When cooking pork, a simple way of making apple sauce is to put one or two apples in along with the joint. When the joint is cooked, the apples are soft and have only to be scraped from their skins and the sauce is ready. — **Mrs Suzanne Sparrow, 109 High Road, East Finchley, London.**

1950s Pamphlet —

STEAK AND KIDNEY DUMPLING

8 oz. Flour
4 oz. Chopped or Minced Suet
½ teaspoonful Salt
1 teaspoonful Baking Powder
½ lb. Sliced Steak
½ lb. Kidney
Seasoning, Water or Milk

This is an excellent dish for a cold day. It is easy to make and economical.

Mix flour, suet, salt, and baking powder to a soft dough with milk or water. Line a greased pudding-bowl with the paste. Cut up the steak and kidney and put into bowl with seasoning to taste; fill up with water or stock; cover with paste; place a greased paper over the bowl and steam for 2½ to 3 hours. Turn out and serve with mashed potatoes.

STEWED TRIPE

2 lb. Boiled Tripe
2 or 3 Boiled Onions
Pepper and Salt
For Sauce — 1½ oz. Margarine, 1½ oz. Flour, 3 gills Tripe Liquor, and 1 gill Milk

Tripe is a valuable article of the diet, especially for those of weak digestion. It requires careful preparation and thorough cooking. First wash and scrape the tripe in several waters. Put it into a pan and cover with cold water, and bring to the boil. Strain off the water, rinse thoroughly, and repeat process three or four times until the tripe smells quite sweet. Then return to the rinsed pan, with cold water to cover; bring slowly to the boil and simmer slowly for 10 to 12 hours, or until the tripe is perfectly tender. It can then be served in various ways, the following being very tasty.

Melt the margarine, add the flour, and cook for a few seconds. Add the liquid and bring to the boil. Cut the tripe in pieces and chop the onion. Reheat in sauce for 30 to 40 minutes. Season well.

SCOTCH STEW

"Easy-To-Prepare Meat Dishes"

1 lb. Stewing Steak
1 Onion, 1 large Carrot, 1 Turnip
4 Good-Sized Potatoes
Salt and Pepper
A little hot Water

Stew with plenty vegetables is a nourishing dinner for the children.

Cut the steak into pieces and brown in a pan in which a little dripping has been melted. Cut into slices the onion, carrot, and turnip. Arrange veg on top of meat; sprinkle with salt and pepper, then add the sliced potatoes until the pan is full. Add a little hot water and simmer slowly for two hours.

JUGGED HARE

Try this – it is very good.

Skin, clean and wash hare, cut it in pieces, and add into a jar with an onion, a bunch of sweet herbs, pepper and salt to taste, and a pint of water. Cover the top of the jar closely, so little steam will escape, otherwise the hare will be dry. Put jar in a saucepan of boiling water and keep it boiling three to four hours. When cooked, put the pieces of hare on a dish, skim off fat from the gravy, thicken with a dessertspoon of cornflour, put gravy into a saucepan to boil, pour it over the hare, and serve with red currant jelly.

WHEN CHOOSING MEAT

When buying meat see that it has red lean and nice white fat. Don't purchase if the lean has a purplish or pale pink tint, or if the fat is yellow.

Good mutton has small bones, and the lean is a dull red; the fat should be firm and white and not too much of it. Bright red flesh points to the meat being freshly killed, and it will be tough unless it is hung, but do not buy flabby, damp mutton.

Don't buy fresh pork in hot weather. Salted pork is seasonable all the year round. Pork should be a delicate pink, and the rind soft, thin, and smooth.

Chapter 18

Mince Is Magic

The Sunday Post ran a competition to find the nation's best mince dish. This wasn't just for the staple mince and tatties, it was an attempt to widen the net and find the best meal made with mince.

It was titled "Mince Is Magic" and 12 finalists were invited to The Normandy Hotel, in Glasgow, where radio and TV personalities Jimmy Mack and Muriel Clark, and The Normandy's head chef Bob Robertson, tested and tasted the mince dishes.

The winner was declared to be Mrs Muriel Crawford, of Fraserburgh, with her Mince Collops. Runner-up was Mrs Jennie McIntyre, of Kilmalcolm, with Savoury Mince With Souffle Topping. In third place was Jessie Thomson, of Glasgow, with Little Bit Different Mince.

It is an honour and a mouthwatering privilege to re-print all 12 shortlisted recipes from that mid-1980s competition, and my thanks and appreciation will forever be owed to all of the finalists.

Mince is, indeed, magic.

The winning recipe from:
MRS MURIEL CRAWFORD, BIGGAR COURT, FRASERBURGH

MINCE COLLOPS

Ingredients: 1 lb. lean minced steak,
2 oz. beef suet,
3 tablespoons finely chopped parsley,
1 egg (beaten), Seasoning, ½ grated onion

Method: Put all the ingredients in a bowl and mix well. Form into 8–10 round flat cakes.

Melt 3 oz. butter or marg. in frying pan until sizzling hot. Dip cakes in flour and then fry until a rich brown on both sides.

If sauce is required, put ½ grated onion into pan in which cakes were cooked. Add a little more butter or marg. if required.

Stir in ½ tablespoon plain flour and cook for 2 mins.

Add either 7 fl. oz. beef stock, 3 fl. oz. red wine or 3 fl. oz. lager. Season with salt, black pepper and bring to boil.

If using lager for sauce add 2 teaspoons malt vinegar, pinch of ground cloves, ½ teaspoon German mustard plus a dash of lemon juice.

Serve with creamed potatoes, fried onions and peas, chopped parsley.

The winning recipe from
MRS MURIEL CRAWFORD, BIGGAR COURT, FRASERBURGH

MINCE COLLOPS

Ingredients:— 1lb lean minced steak,
2 oz. beef suet,
3 tablespoons finely chopped parsley,
1 egg (beaten),
Seasoning,
½ grated onion

Method:— Put all the ingredients in a bowl and mix well. Form into 8-10 round flat cakes.
Melt 3 oz. butter or marg in frying pan until sizzling hot. Dip cakes in flour and then fry until rich brown on both sides.
If sauce IS required, put ½ grated onion into pan in which cakes were cooked. Add a little more butter or marg if required.
Stir in ½ tablespoon plain flour and cook for 2 mins.
Add either 7 fl. oz. beef stock, 3 fl. oz. red wine or 3 fl. oz. lager. Season with salt, black pepper and bring to boil.
If using lager for sauce add 2 teaspoons malt vinegar, pinch of ground cloves, ½ teaspoon German mustard plus a dash of lemon juice.
Serve with creamed potatoes, fried onions and peas, chopped parsley.

Mrs Crawford, who's married with a 10-year-old son, Martin, confessed the recipe owes a lot to Lord Boothby.
As Bob Boothby, he was MP for East Aberdeenshire from 1924 to 1958.
Mrs Crawford was helping out in a hotel when he phoned to book a meal and asked specially for mince collops.
The chef had never heard of them, but he phoned around and soon came up with a recipe which the MP enjoyed.
A very young Mrs Crawford took careful note!
When she read of our contest, she raked around the house until she found it.

The runner-up recipe from:
MRS JENNIE McINTYRE, DIPPANY FARM, KILMALCOLM

SAVOURY MINCE WITH SOUFFLE TOPPING

Ingredients: 16 oz. minced steak
1 small green pepper
1 small onion
2 oz. mushrooms
2 large tomatoes
1 tablespoon oil
Pinch of mixed herbs
Seasoning
For the soufflé topping: 2 oz. finely chopped or grated cheese
3 tablespoons evaporated milk
2 eggs
Salt and pepper
Sprig of parsley

The runner-up was
MRS JENNIE McINTYRE, DIPPANY FARM, KILMALCOLM

SAVOURY MINCE WITH SOUFFLE TOPPING

Ingredients:— 16 oz. minced steak
1 small green pepper
1 small onion
2 oz. mushrooms
2 large tomatoes
1 tablespoon oil
Pinch of mixed herbs
Seasoning

For the souffle topping:— 2 oz. finely chopped or grated cheese
3 tablespoons evaporated milk
2 eggs
Salt and pepper
Sprig of parsley

Method:— Chop the pepper, removing seeds and core. Skin and chop the onion. Skin and slice the mushrooms and tomatoes.
Heat the oil and lightly fry all the veg. until onion is golden brown.
Place the minced steak in an ovenproof dish and top it with the veg.
Sprinkle seasonings on top.
Make souffle by melting the cheese in evaporated milk in a basin over hot water. Allow to cool slightly.
Stir in egg yolks.
Whisk egg whites stiffly then fold into cheese mixture and seasoning. Place on top of meat and veg.
Bake until souffle is well risen and lightly browned (about 20-25 minutes).
Serve quickly, garnished with parsley.

Method: Chop the pepper, removing seeds and core. Skin and chop the onion. Skin and slice the mushrooms and tomatoes.

Heat the oil and lightly fry all the veg. until onion is golden brown. Place the minced steak in an ovenproof dish and top it with the veg. Sprinkle seasonings on top.

Make soufflé by melting the cheese in evaporated milk in a basin over hot water. Allow to cool slightly. Stir in egg yolks.

Whisk egg whites stiffly then fold into cheese mixture and seasoning. Place on top of meat and veg.

Bake until soufflé is well risen and lightly browned (about 20 – 25 minutes). Serve quickly, garnished with parsley.

In Third Place was:
JESSIE THOMSON, 25 KINGSBRIDGE CRESCENT, GLASGOW

LITTLE BIT DIFFERENT MINCE

Ingredients: 1 lb. shoulder steak mince
½ lb. sweetcure bacon
1 thick slice wholemeal bread
2 teaspoons finely chopped parsley
Pinch of salt and pepper

Method: Mix together minced steak, wholemeal breadcrumbs and chopped parsley, plus salt and pepper.

Roll up tablespoons of mixture in slices of bacon. Place the mince and bacon "parcels" in casserole. Add 2 tblsp. of water.

Bake in pre-heated oven, 180° C., 350° F., Regulo 4 for 1 hour.

For party occasions, serve with a thick, creamy cheese sauce, lightly flavoured with basil.

In Third Place was
JESSIE THOMSON, 25 KINGSBRIDGE CRES., GLASGOW

LITTLE BIT DIFFERENT MINCE

Ingredients:— 1 lb. shoulder steak mince
½ lb. sweetcure bacon
1 thick slice wholemeal bread
2 teaspoons finely chopped parsley
Pinch of salt and pepper

Method:— Mix together minced steak, wholemeal breadcrumbs and chopped parsley, plus salt and pepper.
Roll up tablespoons of mixture in slices of bacon. Place the mince and bacon "parcels" in casserole. Add 2 tblsp. of water.
Bake in pre-heated oven, 180° C., 350° F., Regulo 4 for 1 hour.
For party occasions, serve with a thick, creamy cheese sauce, lightly flavoured with basil.

Jessie's recipe — mince and bacon parcels baked in the oven — dates back to the days of the Second World War, when a little meat had to go a long way.

Jessie was a student at a teacher training college when the dish was served up.

She liked it so much, she worked out this recipe of her own.

From MRS WIN MACLEAN, 4 BALBIRNIE PLACE, WESTER COATES, EDINBURGH.

BOSNIAN MEATBALLS

Ingredients: 1 lb. mince
1 onion, finely chopped
2 ozs. flour
2 cloves of garlic, crushed
1 egg
Salt and pepper
Sauce: - 2 eggs
½ pint natural yoghurt
1 teasp. crushed caraway seeds
Salt and pepper

Method: Mix the mince, onion and garlic with the egg, flour and seasoning. Knead well and roll into small balls once you've floured your hands.

Bake on large tray in centre of oven (190° C., 375° F., Regulo 5) for 30 minutes.

Transfer balls to flat heatproof dish and cover with the sauce, prepared by beating the ingredients together. Cover with lid.

Reduce oven temperature to 170°/Mark 3 and cook for 20-30 minutes until sauce thickens like curd around the meatballs.

Serve with rice, green salad or pitta bread.

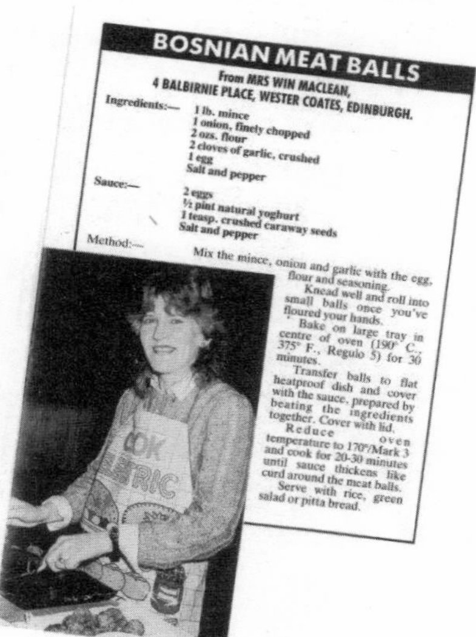

BOSNIAN MEAT BALLS

From MRS WIN MACLEAN,
4 BALBIRNIE PLACE, WESTER COATES, EDINBURGH.

Ingredients:— 1 lb. mince
1 onion, finely chopped
2 ozs. flour
2 cloves of garlic, crushed
1 egg
Salt and pepper

Sauce:— 2 eggs
½ pint natural yoghurt
1 teasp. crushed caraway seeds
Salt and pepper

Method:— Mix the mince, onion and garlic with the egg, flour and seasoning.

Knead well and roll into small balls once you've floured your hands.

Bake on large tray in centre of oven (190° C., 375° F., Regulo 5) for 30 minutes.

Transfer balls to flat heatproof dish and cover with the sauce, prepared by beating the ingredients together. Cover with lid.

Reduce oven temperature to 170°/Mark 3 and cook for 20-30 minutes until sauce thickens like curd around the meat balls.

Serve with rice, green salad or pitta bread.

From MRS MAVIS OGILVIE, 5 ABBEY GARDENS, COUPAR ANGUS

APPLE AND NUT MEAT LOAF

Ingredients: ¾ lb. lean steak mince
1 medium cooking apple (grated)
4 tbls. unsweetened apple juice
2 oz. cooked brown rice
2 oz. chopped salted peanuts
½ teasp. dried rosemary
Salt and pepper

Barbecued apple sauce: 1 tbl. oil
1 finely chopped onion
1 tbl. dark brown sugar
2 tbls. tomato sauce
2–3 drops tabasco sauce
½ pint unsweetened apple juice

APPLE AND NUT MEAT LOAF

From MRS MAVIS OGILVIE, 5 ABBEY GARDENS, COUPAR ANGUS

Ingredients:— ¾ lb. lean steak mince
4 tbls. unsweetened apple juice
2 oz. cooked brown rice
1 medium-sized cooking apple (grated)
2 oz. chopped salted peanuts
½ teasp. dried rosemary
Salt and pepper.

Method:— Combine all the ingredients and press into lined 1 lb. loaf tin.
Bake for one hour at 200° C., 400° F. or Regulo 6.
Serve hot with barbecued apple sauce and piped creamed potatoes OR cold on bed of lettuce garnished with red apple and a few peanuts.

BARBECUED APPLE SAUCE

1 tbl. oil
1 finely chopped onion
1 tbl. dark brown sugar
2 tbls. tomato sauce
2-3 drops tabasco sauce
½ pint unsweetened apple juice

Fry onion in oil until transparent. Add sugar, tomato sauce and tabasco sauce.
Cook for a few minutes. Gradually add apple juice and simmer for 15 minutes.
Liquidise sauce if wished.

Method: Combine all the ingredients and press into lined 1 lb. loaf tin. Bake for one hour at 200° C., 400° F. or Regulo 6.

Serve hot with barbecued apple sauce and piped creamed potatoes OR cold on bed of lettuce garnished with red apple and a few peanuts.

Apple sauce: Fry onion in oil until transparent. Add sugar, tomato sauce and tabasco sauce.

Cook for a few minutes. Gradually add apple juice and simmer for 15 minutes.

Liquidise sauce if wished.

From ROBERT ROBERTSON, 23 TEVIOT PLACE, CAMBUSLANG

MINCIE BREW

Ingredients: 1 lb. mince
2 large onions (finely chopped and fried in soya sauce).
1 chicken cube
1 bay leaf
1 tin peeled tomatoes plus salt and black pepper
1 tbl. tomato puree
1 pinch mixed herbs
1 pinch dried parsley
4 fl. ozs. McEwan's export
1½ teasp. plain flour
1 clove garlic

MINCIE BREW

From ROBERT ROBERTSON, 23 TEVIOT PLACE, CAMBUSLANG.

Ingredients:— 1 lb. mince
2 large onions (finely chopped and fried in soya sauce).
1 chicken cube
1 bay leaf
1 tin peeled tomatoes plus salt and black pepper
1 tbl. tomato puree
1 pinch mixed herbs
1 pinch dried parsley
4 fl. ozs. McEwan's export
1½ teasp. plain flour
1 clove garlic

Method:— Brown mince. Chop onions finely and fry, adding soya sauce.
Drain mince and add salt and pepper, chicken cube and bay leaf.
Mix peeled tomatoes with puree then add to mince. Also add onions to mince once they're soft.
Whilst stirring, add herbs, parsley and crushed garlic. When fully mixed, add export and plain flour. Stir well.
Cover saucepan and simmer for 25 minutes, stirring occasionally.

Method: Brown mince. Chop onions finely and fry, adding soya sauce.

Drain mince and add salt and pepper, chicken cube and bay leaf.

Mix peeled tomatoes with puree then add to mince. Also add onions to mince once they're soft.

Whilst stirring, add herbs, parsley and crushed garlic. When fully mixed, add export and plain flour.

Stir well.

Cover saucepan and simmer for 25 minutes, stirring occasionally.

From ANN MACAULAY, 43 ALMOND AVENUE, DEAN PARK, RENFREW

ALLIGATOR STEW

Ingredients: 1 lb. mince
4 large onions
1 large tin baked beans
1 tin tomato soup
1 tbl. soft brown sugar

Method: Prepare onions and cut into slices.
Take pieces of mince and roll into balls about the size of a medium egg.

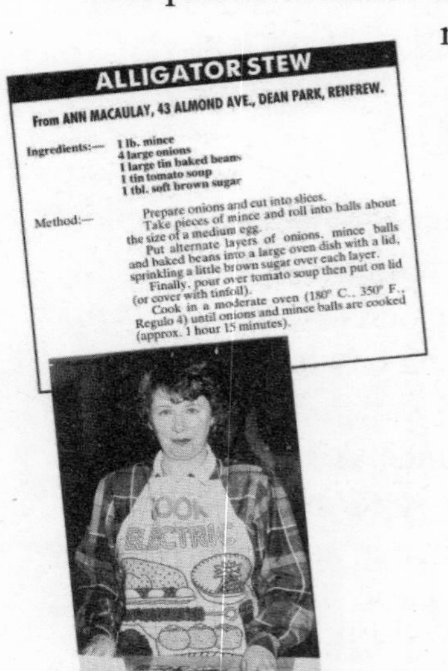

ALLIGATOR STEW

From ANN MACAULAY, 43 ALMOND AVE., DEAN PARK, RENFREW.

Ingredients:— 1 lb. mince
4 large onions
1 large tin baked beans
1 tin tomato soup
1 tbl. soft brown sugar

Method:— Prepare onions and cut into slices.
Take pieces of mince and roll into balls about the size of a medium egg.
Put alternate layers of onions, mince balls and baked beans into a large oven dish with a lid, sprinkling a little brown sugar over each layer.
Finally, pour over tomato soup then put on lid (or cover with tinfoil).
Cook in a moderate oven (180° C., 350° F., Regulo 4) until onions and mince balls are cooked (approx. 1 hour 15 minutes).

Put alternate layers of onions, mince balls and baked beans into a large oven dish with a lid, sprinkling a little brown sugar over each layer.

Finally, pour over tomato soup then put on lid (or cover with tinfoil).

Cook in a moderate oven (180° C., 350° F., Regulo 4) until onions and mince balls are cooked (approx. 1 hour 15 minutes).

From NORRIE GRAHAM, WESTERN AVENUE, RUTHERGLEN

SPECIAL BEEF BOLOGNESE

Ingredients: 1 small tin tomato puree
½ can plum tomatoes
Pinch of mixed herbs (thyme, parsley, cut bay leaves, marjoram)
¾ pint water
½ teaspoon Garlic salt
¼ teaspoon chilli powder
1 Oxo cube
1 heaped tablespoon plain flour
2 teaspoons brown sugar
A sprinkle of Parmesan cheese
Pinch of black pepper

SPECIAL BEEF BOLOGNESE

FROM NORRIE GRAHAM, WESTERN AVE., RUTHERGLEN

Ingredients:— 1 small tin tomato puree
½ can plum tomatoes
Pinch of mixed herbs (thyme, parsley, cut bay leaves, marjoram)
¾ pint water
½ teaspoon Garlic salt
¼ teaspoon chilli powder
1 Oxo cube
1 heaped tablespoon plain flour
2 teaspoons brown sugar
A sprinkle of Parmesan cheese
Pinch of black pepper

Method:— Blend above ingredients together in a blender for 30 seconds.

Take ¾ lb. best steak mince and brown in 2 oz. of butter, put the mince and the ingredients from the blender into a large saucepan, add 2 bay leaves and simmer for half an hour.

For Serving:—

Cook 8 oz. spaghetti in a large saucepan to which 3 pints water, 1 teaspoon salt, ½ teaspoon turmeric, dash vegetable oil have been added.

Boil for about 10 minutes.

Strain spaghetti, add knob of butter.

Put spaghetti on the plates sprinkle with Parmesan cheese, pour the sauce over spaghetti and sprinkle again with Parmesan cheese.

Method: Blend above ingredients together in a blender for 30 seconds. Take ¾ lb. best steak mince and brown in 2 oz. of butter, put the mince and the ingredients from the blender into a large saucepan, add 2 bay leaves and simmer for half an hour.

For Serving: Cook 8 oz. spaghetti in a large saucepan to which 3 pints water, 1 teaspoon salt, ½ teaspoon turmeric, dash vegetable oil have been added.

Boil for about 10 minutes.

Strain spaghetti, add knob of butter.

Put spaghetti on the plates, sprinkle with Parmesan cheese, pour the sauce over spaghetti and sprinkle again with Parmesan cheese.

From MRS MOLLY KENNEDY, 1B CHURCH TERRACE, TARBERT, ARGYLL

ARGYLL VENISON MINCE

Ingredients: 1lb. minced venison
2 dessertspoons butter or margarine
1 chopped onion
1 heaped tablespoon plain flour
Salt and pepper to taste
½ cup red wine

Method: Lightly brown mince and onion in pan with the butter or marg. for 15 minutes.

When browned, add red wine, salt and pepper.

Stir all together, add a little water if necessary, then thicken with the plain flour mixed in cold water to a cream.

Cook for another 5 minutes.

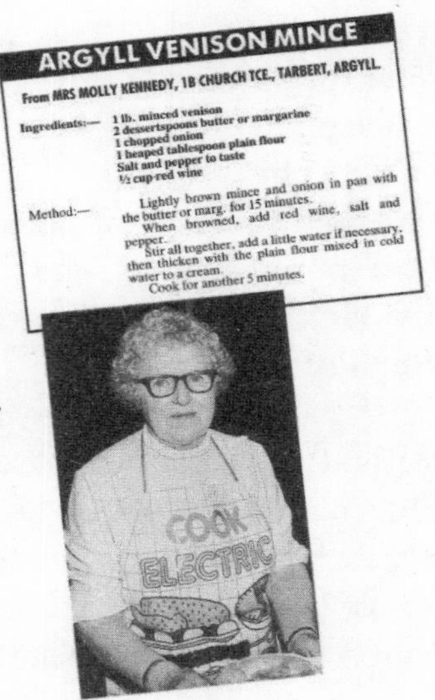

ARGYLL VENISON MINCE

From MRS MOLLY KENNEDY, 1B CHURCH TCE., TARBERT, ARGYLL.

Ingredients:— 1 lb. minced venison
2 dessertspoons butter or margarine
1 chopped onion
1 heaped tablespoon plain flour
Salt and pepper to taste
½ cup red wine

Method:— Lightly brown mince and onion in pan with the butter or marg. for 15 minutes.
When browned, add red wine, salt and pepper.
Stir all together, add a little water if necessary, then thicken with the plain flour mixed in cold water to a cream.
Cook for another 5 minutes.

From MRS SHEILA STEWART, 9 CASTLE ROAD, NEWTON MEARNS, GLASGOW

MINCE DIANE

Ingredients: 1 lb. steak mince
1 onion
1 small green pepper
1 small red pepper
3 chillis
4 ozs. long grain rice

MINCE DIANE

From MRS SHEILA STEWART, 9 CASTLE ROAD, NEWTON MEARNS, GLASGOW.

Ingredients:— 1 lb. steak mince
1 onion
1 small green pepper
1 small red pepper
3 chillis
4 ozs. long grain rice

Method:— Boil rice in salt water for 20 minutes. Wash and dry.

Store in a dish to keep it warm.

Cook mince till tender.

Fry onion, peppers and chillis in butter and oil until tender. Add to mince and simmer for another 20 minutes.

Season well with salt and pepper.

Add 2 dessertspoons of gravy mix. When ready to serve, stir in 2 dessertspoons of single cream.

Serve on a bed of rice.

Method: Boil rice in salt water for 20 minutes. Wash and dry.

Store in a dish to keep it warm.

Cook mince till tender.

Fry onion, peppers and chillis in butter and oil until tender. Add to mince and simmer for another 20 minutes.

Season well with salt and pepper.

Add 2 dessertspoons of gravy mix. When ready to serve, stir in 2 dessertspoons of single cream.

Serve on a bed of rice.

From MRS ANNE LAING, PAVILION COTTAGE, MELROSE

MINCE AU GRATIN

Ingredients: 1 oz. butter
1 large onion
12 ozs. mince
14 ozs. canned tomatoes
2 tablespoons dry sherry
½ teaspoon thyme
1 bay leaf
Salt and pepper
1 lb. packet frozen spinach
6 ozs. noodles
2 teasp. cornflour
¾ pint cheese sauce
2 knobs butter
Crushed clove of garlic.

MINCE AU GRATIN

From MRS ANNE LAING, PAVILION COTTAGE, MELROSE.

Ingredients:— 1 oz. butter
1 large onion
12 ozs. mince
14 ozs. canned tomatoes
2 tablespoons dry sherry
½ teaspoon thyme
1 bay leaf
Salt and pepper
1 lb. packet frozen spinach
6 ozs. noodles
2 teasp. cornflour
¾ pint cheese sauce
2 knobs butter
Crushed clove of garlic

Method:— Heat 1 oz. of butter and fry onion (chopped). Add mince and cook.

Stir in tomatoes, add sherry, garlic etc., and seasoning. Simmer for 30-45 minutes.

Heat spinach with a knob of butter. Drain well and spread over base of ovenproof dish.

Cook noodles in boiling salted water. Drain, then add remaining knob of butter.

Blend cornflour in water and stir into mince and tomato mixture and bring to boil.

Adjust seasoning, spoon half cheese sauce over spinach, top with noodles, meat sauce and finally rest of cheese sauce.

Sprinkle 2 ozs. cheese on top.

Heat thoroughly in oven at 160° C., 325° F., Gas Mark 3 for 30 minutes.

Method: Heat 1oz. of butter and fry onion (chopped). Add mince and cook.

Stir in tomatoes, add sherry, garlic etc., and seasoning. Simmer for 30 – 45 minutes.

Heat spinach with a knob of butter. Drain well and spread over base of ovenproof dish.

Cook noodles in boiling salted water. Drain, then add remaining knob of butter.

From MRS LYDIA A. SHARP, BIRCHWOOD AVENUE, WOODLANDS PARK, NORTH GOSFORTH, NEWCASTLE

MEXICAN SPICED MINCE BEEF

Ingredients: 1 lb. mince
1 small tin pineapples
1 small tin tomatoes
1 medium onion
1 green pepper
2 tbls. sherry
2 tbls. soya sauce
1 tbls. ground ginger

Method: Fry onion and mince until brown.

Add juice from pineapples.

Add tomatoes, sherry, soya sauce and ground ginger and simmer for 30 minutes.

Add green pepper and chopped pineapple. Save some for top and cook for further 15 minutes.

Serve with boiled rice or spaghetti.

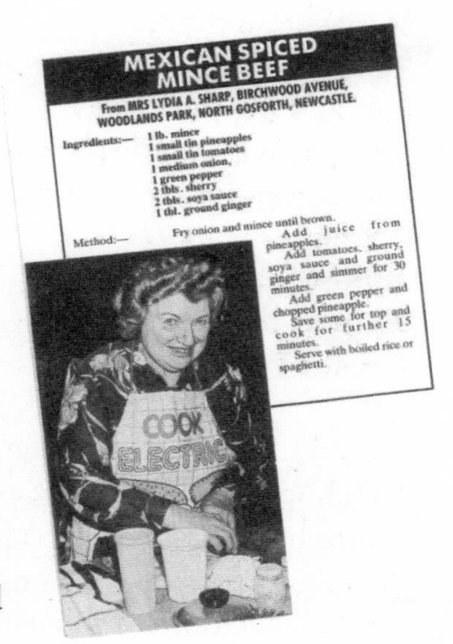
MEXICAN SPICED MINCE BEEF

From MRS LYDIA A. SHARP, BIRCHWOOD AVENUE, WOODLANDS PARK, NORTH GOSFORTH, NEWCASTLE.

Ingredients:— 1 lb. mince
1 small tin pineapples
1 small tin tomatoes
1 medium onion,
1 green pepper
2 tbls. sherry
2 tbls. soya sauce
1 tbl. ground ginger

Method:— Fry onion and mince until brown.
Add juice from pineapples.
Add tomatoes, sherry, soya sauce and ground ginger and simmer for 30 minutes.
Add green pepper and chopped pineapple.
Save some for top and cook for further 15 minutes.
Serve with boiled rice or spaghetti.

And the competitions kept coming. It's always worth looking at the secret recipe of a competition winner —

TABLET COMPETITION

The Sunday Post

TABLET COMPETITION

Our winner was **Mrs Jessie Fairns from Beith, Ayrshire.**
Here's her recipe:-
Ingredients
1 teacupful whole milk
2 oz. Lurpak butter
2 lb. granulated sugar
Small tin of Nestlés condensed milk
1 tablespoon syrup
Few drops vanilla essence.

Method

Put the milk, sugar and butter in a strong pan.
Once the butter is melted and sugar dissolved, add the condensed milk.
Bring slowly to the boil, stirring all the time.
Add the syrup and boil gently for 5 minutes.
Test the mixture by putting a teaspoonful in a cup of cold water. If it is firm and holding together, take the pot off the heat.
Add the vanilla essence and beat for 3 to 5 minutes.
Pour the mixture into a tray and allow to cool.

OUR winner was Mrs Jessie Fairns from Beith, Ayrshire.

Here's her recipe: -

Ingredients
1 teacupful Whole Milk
2 oz. Lurpak Butter
2 lb. Granulated Sugar
Small tin of Nestlés Condensed Milk
1 tablespoon Syrup
Few drops Vanilla Essence

Method:

Put the milk, sugar and butter in a strong pan.

Once the butter is melted and sugar dissolved, add the condensed milk.

Bring slowly to the boil, stirring all the time.

Add the syrup and boil gently for 5 minutes.

Test the mixture by putting a teaspoonful in a cup of cold water. If it is firm and holding together, take the pot off the heat.

Add the vanilla essence and beat for 3 to 5 minutes.

Pour the mixture into a tray and allow to cool.

CHAMPION STOVIES

STOVIES is a traditional Scottish dish – stove simply means to stew or simmer.

It started life in the kitchens of big country houses. The cooks used the dripping from the Sunday roast, potatoes and onions, always to hand, to make a filling dish for the downstairs staff.

Jane Galbraith, The Sunday Post/Potato Marketing Board stovie champion, uses a traditional recipe.

It's easy to make. You need only 10 minutes' preparation and half an hour cooking time.

For four, you'll need
2 oz. dripping,
1½ lbs. potatoes
two or three onions.

The Sunday Post

CHAMPION STOVIES!

STOVIES is a traditional Scottish dish—stove simply means to stew or simmer.

It started life in the kitchens of big country houses. The cooks used the dripping from the Sunday roast, potatoes and onions, always to hand, to make a filling dish for the downstairs staff.

Jane Galbraith, The Sunday Post/Potato Marketing Board stovie champion uses a traditional recipe.

It's easy to make. You need only 10 minutes' preparation and half an hour cooking time.

For four, you'll need 2 oz dripping, one and a half pounds of potatoes and two or three onions.

Melt the dripping and fry the onions in it, peel and slice the potatoes, and add to the dripping and onions.

Cover and cook for about 30 minutes.

The stovies are ready when the tatties are tender, whole but just about to fall. Jane's recipe is very traditional.

Some people add a little water with the potatoes and cook the stovies in the steam.

Over the years, stovies have evolved. Nowadays lots of ingredients are added. Most common is left-over cooked meat—could be beef or lamb.

In the Borders, stovies were traditionally served with soup beforehand, or with a glass of buttermilk.

In the North East, fish is often added to make a sort of fish stew. Or by adding milk, a thick soup.

In the Highlands and Islands, potatoes and limpets are layered to make limpet stovies. You can do the same with chicken.

There are endless variations to an inexpensive and easy-to-make dish.

□ Jane Galbraith with Jimmie Macgregor, Bob Meredith, manager of Marketing and Research for P.M.B. and Bill Anderson, Editor of The Sunday Post.

Melt the dripping and fry the onions in it, peel and slice the potatoes, and add to the dripping and onions.

Cover and cook for about 30 minutes.

The stovies are ready when the tatties are tender, whole but just about to fall. Jane's recipe is very traditional. Some people add a little water with the potatoes and cook the stovies in the steam.

Over the years, stovies have evolved. Nowadays lots of ingredients are added. Most common is left-over cooked meat — could be beef or lamb.

In the Borders, stovies were traditionally served with soup beforehand, or with a glass of buttermilk.

In the North East, fish is often added to make a sort of fish stew. Or by adding milk, a thick soup.

In the Highlands and Islands, potatoes and limpets are layered to make limpet stovies. You can do the same with chicken.

There are endless variations to an inexpensive and easy-to-make dish.

Chapter 19

Give Us This Day...

PERHAPS surprisingly, bread was never rationed during the war, although there was a short period when it was on the ration card in the late 1940s, due to the weather ruining the wheat crop. But, for the most part, even in the severe rationing period following 1945, you could buy bread — if you had the money and if the baker you were registered with had any.

One of the reasons for unrationed bread was that bakers had to use National Flour and make only one type. This was named The National Loaf.

Nutritionists were impressed with the healthy composition of The National Loaf and after the war even fought for it to be the only type of bread it was legal to make in Britain. The population, though, wasn't quite so keen. The National Loaf was nicknamed "Hitler's Secret Weapon".

However, tasty or not, Government formula flour and baking restrictions kept bread on kitchen tables.

Perhaps surprisingly, not many households baked their own, probably because it isn't an easy thing to do.

Ordinary folk were more interested in another problem with bread — the best way to fry it.

December 9, 1951.
TASTY — Before frying bread, soften it with warm water. It will be light and tasty instead of hard and greasy. — **Mrs G. Jobes, 56 Bridgegate, Irvine.**

FOOD NEWS **November 5, 1950.**

Bake Your Own

I AGREE with the reader who complained about the dreary bread we get nowadays.

I buy three pounds of wholemeal flour. I follow the directions printed on the bag and with little trouble, make enough excellent bread for my family of three for a week.

Perhaps if more housewives made their own bread, the authorities would do something about the stuff in the shops.
— **Mrs K. Stenport, 60 Bellshill Road, Glasgow.**

January 20, 1952.
BACON — Fried bread can be made more attractive by cutting small rounds with a fluted pastry cutter. Spread one side with meat or vegetable extract, sandwich two together, dip in milk and fry till golden brown. Serve with fried bacon. — **H. Ostler, 22 Henderson Park, Windygates, Fife.**

September 30, 1956.
FRYING — Before frying bread, damp both sides of the slice. This gives an even brownness and crispness. — **Mrs W. Wright, Oatlands, 130 Arthur Street, Dunfermline.**

March 3, 1957.
MINCER — Don't throw away crusts of bread. Crisp them up in the oven, then put them through the mincer. This sharpens the blades, and the crumbs do for fish dressing. — **Mrs Lilly, 37 Johnston Avenue, Dundee.**

July 14, 1957.

FRIED BREAD — To prevent fried bread from being fat-sodden, don't put any fat in the pan. Simply spread the slice of bread lightly on both sides with margarine before popping it into a dry pan. It will toast to a dry, golden brown. — **Mrs R. Symon, The Pearce Institute, Pearce Street, Glasgow, S.W.1.**

Brown & Polson
Flavoured Cornflour for
fruity-flavoured blancmanges
...and lots of other
lovely things like
CARAMEL
COCONUT PUDDING
Quick to make! Delicious both hot and cold! For a hot pudding take the Caramel envelope in a 5-flavour packet of Brown & Polson Flavoured Cornflour and make a cornflour cream pudding as directed on the packet. (For a cold pudding use 1 pint milk.) stir in some desiccated coconut, pour into serving dish and sprinkle with more coconut. If desired, brown before serving.
5 FLAVOURS IN
ONE PACKET
1/2½d

August 18, 1957.
SANDWICHES — When making sandwiches, butter each slice before cutting, especially if the bread is to be cut thinly. — **Mrs R. Martin, 20a Somerville Place, Carstairs Junction.**

August 25, 1957.
SOUPS AND STEWS — To absorb excess grease from the top of soups and stews, place a slice of fresh bread on the surface. Remove before serving. — **Jessie Ross, 28 Cambridge Road, Huddersfield.**

November 16, 1958.
SUBSTITUTE — When a recipe calls for breadcrumbs, you can use cornflakes instead. Saves time, too. — **Mrs J. Brown, 64 Grange Estate, Church Crookham, near Aldershot.**

March 22, 1959.
BROWN BREAD — When bread is baked, turn off the oven, slip the bread out of the tin and return it to the cooling oven for another ten minutes or so. The outside turns to a delicious golden crispness. The inside retains its soft sponginess. The extra bit of cooking without the tin ensures that the loaf is thoroughly dried out. — **Mrs Mary Hamilton, 134 Cannon Lane, Pinner.**

November 22, 1959.
FRIED BREAD — To make evenly browned slices, spread one side with dripping and fry in hot pan. Then spread the other side and fry. — **Mrs D. Goodwin, 1 Portland Drive, Dumfries.**

December 6, 1959.
CATCH THE JUICE — When next you grill kidneys or steak, place a few thick slices of bread under the rack of the griller to catch the juice. When the meat is ready, toast the bread for a few seconds and serve under the meat or kidneys. — **M. Wilson, Beach Cliffe, 409 Warbreck Drive, Bispham, Blackpool.**

Chapter 20

Christmas Fare

CHRISTMAS Dinner used to hold a more elevated place in the line up of festive attractions. Before TV specials of our favourite sitcoms, before time off work (working people didn't get a day off for Christmas) and even before it became compulsory to spend far too much money on toys kids don't need or even really want...the food was the highlight of the celebrations.

Ordinary folk didn't sit down to a turkey with all the trimmings, or a goose at any other time of year. Even a roast chicken was a rare treat.

Christmas was a celebration for your appetite...but The Sunday Post's Doc had words of warning too.

THE DOC REPLIES **December 10, 1950.**

Now, About That Xmas Dumpling

Is it OK from the medical point of view to put threepenny bits in the Christmas dumpling?

Yes, but don't wrap them in paper. They're apt to carry germs that way. And scrub them well before putting them in. I don't favour the use of sharp "charms" like bells, &c., in the dumpling, in case they accidentally get into the mouth.

FOOD NEWS **September 21, 1952.**

CHRISTMAS FRUITS

CURRANTS and sultanas will form the dried fruit allocation for Christmas.

It's a good one and will be in the shops next period.

There's more tinned milk in the shops. But be quick, for the demand is still brisk. Prices, sweetened and unsweetened, from 1s1d to 1s7d a tin.

Some bananas are still available, and more are on the way. A cargo is due at Hull this week.

Another allocation of "Skippers" — one of the few since the war — is expected soon.

I now find the canned fruits mentioned two weeks ago come from Northern Ireland, not Eire. The canning is done from fresh pears, fruit salad, peaches, grapefruit, and apricots, which come direct from California to the canneries.

December 12, 1954.
SCORCHED CAKE — If your Christmas cake is scorched, scrape off the dark patches with a fine grater, then paint over with white of egg. Put back into a moderate oven for a few minutes. — **Mrs C. Graham, 180 Brooms Road, Dumfries.**

August 7, 1955.
CHRISTMAS DINNER — To have a supply of new potatoes for Christmas dinner, lift them from the ground, shake off the earth, place in an air-tight tin and bury it under a foot of earth. Lift on Christmas morning. — **Mrs D. King, Northward, Newmachar.**

December 23, 1956.
YULETIDE LOG — Make some suet crust, roll out thinly, and spread with layer of mincemeat, leaving ½ inch paste all round. Moisten edges with water, roll up, and put in a straight 2 lb. jam jar, well greased. Cover with greaseproof paper and steam for two hours. Serve with custard sauce. — **Mrs Slater, 17 Geddes Avenue, Portknockie.**

December 23, 1956.
DOUBLE MINCEMEAT — Chop two sweet apples with a handful each of currants and sultanas, grate a lemon or orange skin, and add two dessertspoons moist sugar. Turn into a large basin a 1 lb. jar of mincemeat. Mix well with above ingredients and fill two jars. — **Mrs R. Paton, 42 Clarence Road, Southport.**

December 8, 1957.
CAKE DECORATION — To make tiny Christmas trees for your Christmas cake, pipe roses of pale green icing one on top of the other, drawing the tip of the top one to a point. Top with a silver cachou or fragment of cherry. — **I. P. Smith, Parkneuk, Arbuthnott, Laurencekirk.**

December 8, 1957.
CHRISTMAS CAKE — If the cake comes out of the oven with a crack on top, cover it immediately with a damp cloth and the crack disappears. — **Mrs S. Hall, 30 Cheviot Road, Chester-le-Street.**

December 15, 1957.
CHRISTMAS FOWL — After the bird is plucked it must be singed. Pour a little methylated spirits on to an old tin plate, and light. Hold the bird over the blue flame. The bird is beautifully white and clean in half the time. — **Mrs E. Foster, 4 North Road, Towlan, Co. Durham.**

December 15, 1957.
FROSTED GRAPES — Frosted grapes make a decorative topping for a cake. Beat one egg white until slightly frothy, and spread it on a bunch of grapes. Sprinkle with granulated sugar. Allow the sugar and egg white to dry. — **Mrs M. Price, 97 Phythian Street, Liverpool.**

December 22, 1957.
DRIED FRUITS — When preparing dried fruit for a Christmas cake, put the cleaned fruit into a bowl. Over the fruit pour the juice of a lemon and the juice of an orange. Leave overnight. This swells the fruit and gives it a delightful flavour. — **Mrs E. Prentice, 110 Hamiltonhill Road, Glasgow.**

December 22, 1957.

NEW FLAVOUR — When making pouring custard for the Christmas pudding, use brown sugar. It gives the sauce a nice caramel flavour. — **(No name), Shangri-La, Lenzie Road, Kirkintilloch.**

December 21, 1958.
KIDDIES PARTY — Stand a swiss roll on end and cover with glace icing, allowing it to run down the sides to look like wax. Tint a piece of marzipan red to represent a flame and stick on top. This candle cake delights the kiddies. — **Mrs F. King, 8 Catherine Street, Doncaster.**

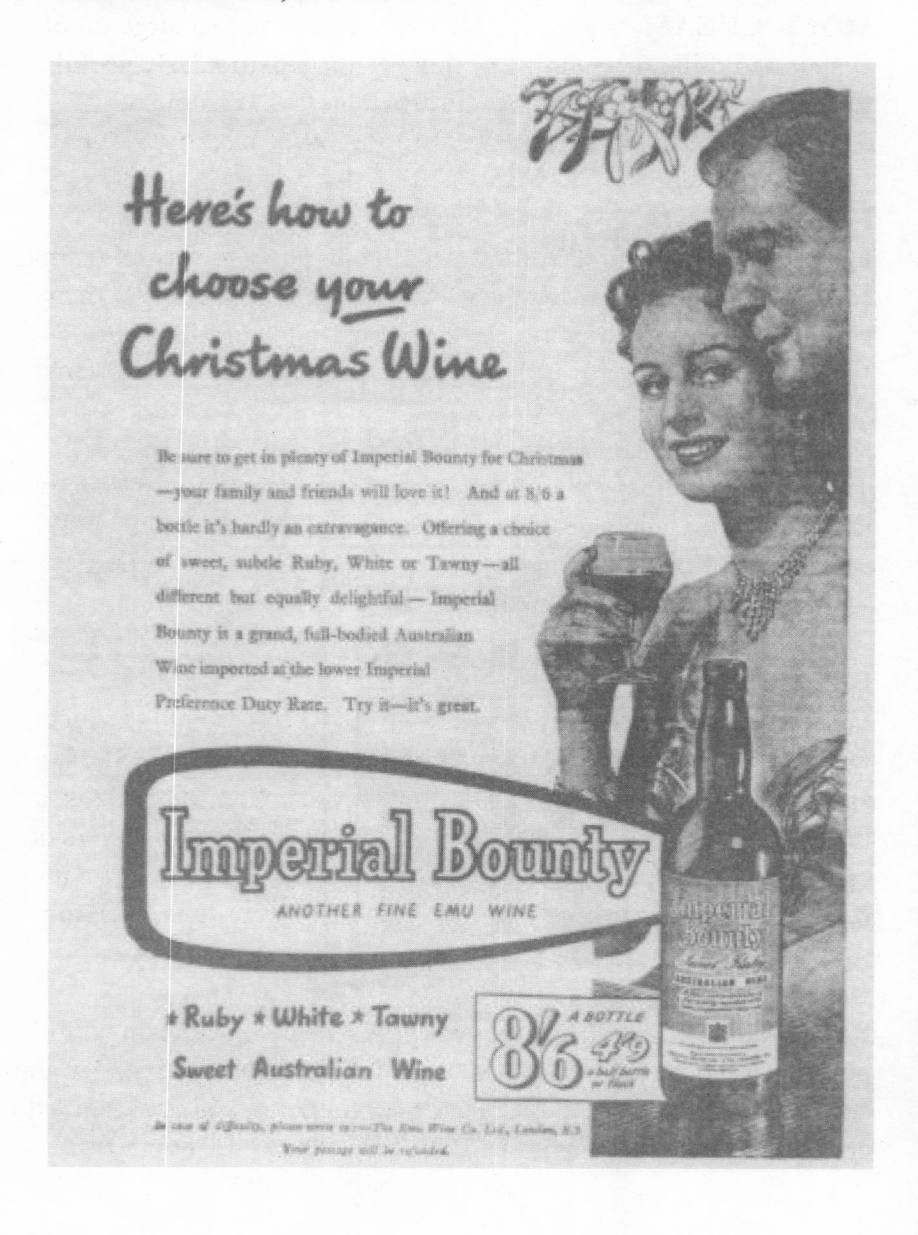

December 28, 1958.
TRIFLE — When making trifle and leaving custard on top, I sprinkle it with caster sugar while still hot. Then no skin forms on top. — **Mrs M. Mailer, Castle Farm, Doune.**

November 15, 1959.
MOCK CREAM — Add the juice of one lemon to a large tin of evaporated milk, mix until very thick. This is particularly useful for children's parties as it goes further than fresh cream and is cheaper. — **Mrs A. Furlong, 9 Bainton Close, Kirkby.**

November 29, 1959.
EXACT SIZE — After rolling out almond paste for my Christmas cake, I use the tin in which the cake was baked as a cutter. I then get the exact size without the bother of cutting and trimming.
— **Miss N. Richmond, Ballytaggart, Ballymoney, Co. Antrim.**

December 13, 1959.
TIT-BIT — Pink apple froth makes a lovely surround for a festive jelly. Peel, core and sweeten apples, cook gently and when cool add the white of an egg and a drop of cochineal. Beat till fluffy.
— **Mrs L. Waugh, 18 Wardlaw Street, Edinburgh.**

December 20, 1959.
FESTIVE FARE — This year at your party, pass round devilled wafers with the drinks. Make a smooth mixture of grated cheese and butter or margarine, some dry mustard, pepper, salt and just a little cayenne pepper to taste. Spread on plain ice-cream wafers or cracker biscuits, put in coolish oven until crisp and keep in tin until required. — **J. Winning, 1 Kensington Park Gardens, London.**

December 20, 1959.
PARTY FARE — Frosted ginger apples make a nice change. Fill peeled and cored baking apples with chopped preserved ginger and sugar. Bake till just tender. Coat with white icing and decorate with crystallised ginger. — **Miss U. Leuchars, Dunain, Inverness.**

Chapter 21
Leftovers

WHEN food was scarce, or the best of it rationed, there weren't many leftovers. It was expected that every plate would be cleared, and woe betide any picky young lad or lass who didn't eat all that was put before them.

But this chapter isn't about leftover food, it is about leftover tips that don't really "fit" in any of the other chapters. They do, however, deserve to be included in the book. Although it might not be a great idea to use asbestos when making toast.

July 9, 1950.
IF HUBBY'S LATE FOR HIS DINNER — If dinner has to be kept warm for someone coming in late, place it on an upper shelf of the oven with the gas turned low. On a shelf beneath place a saucer or shallow bowl filled with water. This will prevent the dinner from becoming dried up. — **Mrs M. Dewhurst, 88 Lytham Road, Fulwood, Preston, wins this week's guinea.**

August 2,1953.
SMOOTH FINISH — Gravy or custard that has gone lumpy is made smooth again by beating for a few minutes with an egg whisk. — **C. Dickson, 192 Govanhill Street, Glasgow.**

there's always time for Nescafé
Nescafé makes such lovely coffee. It has the real roaster-fresh smell, and full and lively flavour. Yet there's none of the bother of making coffee the hard way! With Nescafé, you simply put a teaspoonful in the cup, add piping-hot water, then milk and sugar to taste. What could be quicker? And no coffee could be nicer!
NESCAFÉ
for grand coffee quickly
ANOTHER OF NESTLÉ'S GOOD THINGS

May 31, 1953.
FLOURING — When flouring foods, put flour and seasoning in greaseproof bag. Drop the food in a few pieces at a time, and a shake of the bag has them ready for the pan. — **Mrs K. Beaton, 576 Crow Road, Glasgow.**

September 27, 1953.
CREAMING — I find it much easier and quicker to cream margarine and sugar together with a potato masher. — **Mrs A. Hunter, 23a Danube Street, Edinburgh.**

October 25, 1953.
NO SMELL — The quickest way to get the smell of fish or onions from the frying pan is to wash the pan thoroughly, then turn it upside down over the flame of a gas stove for a few seconds. — **Mrs Mannion, 10 Chesser Avenue, Edinburgh.**

March 21, 1954.
SALT — Before opening a packet of cooking salt, hammer all round with a rolling-pin. This breaks up the lumps and makes it easier to use. — **Mrs J. I. Tait, 23 Burgh Road, Lerwick, Shetland.**

September 5, 1954.
SANDWICHES — When packing sandwiches for a journey, make them up into several small packets instead of one large one. This avoids waste, as food not consumed remains unopened and fresh. — **Mrs G. Tyson, 14 Prince Arthur Road, London.**

May 9, 1954.
COOKERY HINT — To measure half a cupful of butter it's easier if you half fill cup with water and drop in butter until water rises to top of cup. Drain off the water and you then have the amount of butter required — without it sticking to the sides of the cup. — **Mrs A. E. Fordyce, The Comers, Midmar, Aberdeen.**

January 23, 1955.
TOAST — If the toasting grill on your cooker is out of order, put an asbestos mat over one of the gas rings. This toasts the bread an even brown. — **Mrs D. Hardie, 6 Backmarch Crescent, Rosyth.**

May 15, 1955.
EASY TO SEE — Arrange spices and seasonings in alphabetical order on your cupboard shelf. I find it easy to get what is wanted in a hurry by this method instead of looking at all the boxes. — **E. Smith, 14 John Street, Ruabon, near Wrexham.**

June 5, 1955.
MINT — Soak chopped mint in lemon juice instead of vinegar. Add a little more sugar than usual, and you will be delighted with the flavour. — **Mrs M. Marks, 8 Jamieson Road, Liverpool.**

July 3, 1955.
QUICK JOB — When in haste to cream butter for sandwiches, pour several drops of boiling water into the butter as you work it with a fork. It creams instantly, and the surplus water separates itself from the butter, and can be poured off. — **H. Parker, 6 Bowmanflat, Larkhall.**

July 10, 1955.
JELLY PRESERVE — This preserve can be eaten with any kind of cold meat and keeps indefinitely. Dissolve a lemon jelly in hot vinegar and stir in two tablespoonfuls of chopped mint. Stir well and pour into small jars. — **Mrs J. Bell, 6 Waverley Park Terrace, Edinburgh.**

February 12, 1956.
KEEPS DRY — To keep salt and pepper running freely in damp weather, place an inverted tumbler over each container. — **M. C. Toye, 14 Netherhill Road, Paisley.**

Yes please!
There's nothing like a
Perfect in their gay foil wrappers
MUNCHMallow
Creamy milk chocolate—yes!—and crispy biscuit—yes!—
and smoothest mallow—yes please!—
what a taste-thrill for only 2½d
From Macdonalds of Glasgow who bake the best biscuits

July 1, 1956.
SPLASH MAT — To prevent grease splashes marking kitchenette wallpaper behind the cooker, slit a large polythene bag and secure with Sellotape. It can be washed down daily. — **Mrs T. Wilson, 27 Essenside Avenue, Drumchapel, Glasgow.**

July 1, 1956.
BREAD — When first cutting into a loaf of bread, save the top or outer slice. Use this as a lid after each cutting, and the bread keeps longer fresh in the bin. — **A. A. Currie, Linden View, Lilliesleaf, by Melrose.**

September 2, 1956.
HOT DISHES — To make best use of the rack over the hotplate for warming plates, keeping dishes hot, &c., place a clean cloth over the plates and dishes to make an improvised "hot closet".
— Mrs W. Wright, 130 Arthur Street, Dunfermline.

September 9, 1956.
KEEPS FOOD HOT — Instead of putting food into the oven to keep hot for latecomers, cover it with a lid or plate and set it over a saucepan of hot water. This keeps the food hot, and at the same time prevents it from drying up. — **Mrs E. Roach, 6 Cairnswell Place, Cambulsang.**

September 9, 1956.
MUSTARD — Next time you mix mustard, add a little drop of salad oil. It will improve the flavour and prevent the mustard from going hard. — **Mrs A. Lonie, William Street, Tayport.**

September 16, 1956.
TASTY TOAST — Mix a little meat extract with butter before spreading on hot toast. It makes a delightful change for tea.
— Mrs M. Bell, 18 Westlands, Sunderland.

May 5, 1957.

SAUCE — To utilise every drop of thick sauce at the bottom of your sauce bottle, add a little vinegar and shake well. — **Mrs R. Reid, 150 Glenalmond Streeet, Glasgow.**

May 19, 1957.
CREAMING MARG — Put a coarse grater in the oven to heat, then grate the margarine into the sugar and beat up while still warm. The margarine slides off the warm metal, and none is wasted. This is especially good if the margarine is kept in a fridge.
— Mrs Wood, 21 Newfoundland Street, Darlington.

December 8, 1957.
RAISINS — Before stoning raisins, rub a little butter on the fingers, and they don't become sticky. — **Mrs Philp, c/o 29 McKinlay Terrace, Loanhead.**

February 16, 1958.
LONGER FRESH — Mustard does not dry up so quickly and keeps fresh longer if a little olive oil is added when making.
— M. Downie, Eaglesfield, Lockerbie.

April 13, 1958.
TABLET — When making home-made tablet, dispense with the wooden spoon method of beating and use the egg whisk instead. It is much quicker and less strenuous. — **Mrs J. Mackenzie, Beaufort Home Farm, by Beauly.**

August 17, 1958.
QUICK — For quickly made, smooth mustard and a tidy mustard pot, put the water in first, not the dry powder. — **Mrs I. Lindsay, 57 Comely Bank Avenue, Edinburgh.**

September 28, 1958.
COOKERY HINT — Keep a sheet of polythene paper inside your cookery book. Lay it across the page you are consulting. The print is easily readable and the book doesn't become soiled. — **Mrs Wm. Gilchrist, 55 Kintillo Drive, Glasgow.**

October 12, 1958.
SKEWERS — To save skewers from getting lost in the kitchen drawer, put them all together on a key ring and hang on a screw hook. — **Miss Gladys Ramsay, Towers Hotel, Ballater.**

November 9, 1958.
MACARONI —When cooking macaroni, put it into a wire strainer and then into pan of boiling water. In this way it doesn't stick to the pan, and is easily lifted out to drain. — **Mrs H. Smith, 29 Queen's Terrace, Ayr.**

January 18, 1959.
SMOOTH BUTTER — If you are trying to soften butter and you're left with a dish of oil as a result of overheating, stand the dish in cold water for a few minutes. Add a teaspoonful of cream and whip till cool. Result — smooth easy-spreading butter. — **Mrs Whitehill, Hamilton, wins a pair of towels.**

February 1, 1959.
BUTTER — In frosty weather place a piece of butter on a plate. Pop the lid of a boiling kettle over it. Butter spreads in a jiffy. — **Mrs E. McFarlane, 6 Slammanan Road, Avonbridge, Falkirk.**

February 22, 1959.
PARTY-TIME — When making large quantities of sandwiches for a party, pour half a pint of boiling milk over one pound of butter in a basin. Cool slightly, then work together with a wooden spoon until of a creamy consistency. This mixture spreads easily, and goes further than solid butter. — **H. E. Bain, Eldenside, Coulter.**

May 31, 1959.
BUTTER — In hot weather, butter is apt to stick to the paper. To prevent this, hold the packet under the cold water tap and run the water over it. The paper comes off clean. — **Mrs M. McLean, 3 Longhill Terrace, Rothesay.**

June 14, 1959.
SALAD CREAM — When making salad cream or mayonnaise, if you first rub the inside of the bowl with a small piece of garlic, it gives it a delicious tang. — **Mrs T. Thornton, 17 Gibraltar Terrace, Dalkeith.**

June 28, 1959.
SAUCES — Instead of making white sauces for fish, &c., I make up a packet of onion soup mixture, using half the quantity of water stated on the packet. For pouring over cauliflower, I use cauliflower soup with a little grated cheese added to it. — **Miss MacGregor, Sutherland Cottage, Keir Street, Dunblane.**

July 5, 1959.
CUSTARD TIP — To avoid a skin forming on custard that isn't for immediate use, add a tablespoonful of cold milk and stir up well before pouring. — **Miss S. McFarlane, South Mains, Maybole.**

July 12, 1959.
TASTIER SAUCE — When chopping mint for sauce, add a little sugar. This makes work easier and quicker and improves the flavour — **Mrs Tingle, 26 Forster Street, Roker, Sunderland.**

July 12, 1959.
TO PREVENT SKIN — To prevent skin forming on porridge, put lid of pan on immediately the cereal comes through the boil. If made the previous night and kept covered, it re-heats better the next morning. — **Mrs M. Burns, Marburn, 12 Fieldsway, Garden Suburb, Oldham.**

November 15, 1959.

SANDWICHES — When making savoury sandwiches with meat, paste, cheese, &c., add a sprinkling of crushed potato crisps with the filling. This makes the sandwiches more interesting and much crisper. — **Mrs M. Craig, 37 Kilburn Street, Belfast.**

Chapter 22

The Future Of Food

IT is human nature to wonder what will happen tomorrow. It is newspaper nature to print those wonderings. It is the present day's nature to look back at predictions of the past and be amused, or shake the head in the wry knowledge that things just didn't work out the way they were planned.

This article on the following pages was printed in The Sunday Post on December 12, 1954, and reports the opinions of experts, or best-guessers...or complete fantasists, connected to the Royal Society of Arts.

Their predictions are, in turn, utopian, ambitious, worrying and puzzling. But they will be no better, or worse, than our own time's attempts to predict what will be happening in the world half a century into the future.

The selection of which predictions to print — these were just a few of many the RSA gathered — reveal what was important to ordinary people in 1954.

That communication (rocket letter post) was first on the agenda is incredibly perceptive and would have been heartening to the many who had relatives in Australia, Canada or the US.

We now have electronic e-communication, of course, that has made the exchange of mail with anyone, anywhere, an instant thing. They knew then, as we know now, that one of the most important things to any human being is the ability to communicate with our loved ones.

We'll All Eat Wood in 2000 A.D.

The Sunday Post, December 12, 1954 — The Royal Society of Arts, in the current issue of their journal (December 1954), publish a summary of the opinions of 184 people in various parts of the world, who entered the society's bi-centenary competition to provide a forecast of a single practical aspect of life on this earth in 46 years' time.

Some of the forecasts are: -

Communications — The rocket letter post will have made return mail to Australia in a single day possible.

Travel — Pedestrians will move quickly along main streets on automatic speed walks. Pavements in main streets will be raised to first-storey level to allow wider roadways for the traffic below. Passengers will board buses from the top deck.

Heat, Light, Power — A single plastic dome will cover London.

House lighting will be provided from fluorescent walls. Domestic heating and ventilation will be controlled by covering each house and garden with a plastic shell entered by an airlock.

Numbers of space stations will be placed around the earth at heights allowing them to nullify gravity. They will provide bases for space explorations and for concentrating solar energy for use on Earth.

Agriculture and Forestry — Sweetcorn and vines will be extensively cultivated in the South of England. Spraying and dusting soil with special preparations at the time of seed sowing will have done away with the need for weeding.

Food — There will be edible acorns and sugar will be made from wood. The use of wood for anything but food will be prohibited in the United States.

A meatless vegetarian diet will have become compulsory to avoid the land waste involved by meat production.

Industry — Advertisements will be projected on to the night sky, and this space will be sold by reference to the position of the stars.

Whales will be kept in captivity, bred and herded like cattle.

Medicine — Hypnotism will be the accepted means of banishing physical and emotional pain. The treatment of wounds will have been made easier by use of transparent medical wrappings.

—oOo—

Enough's as gude as a feast

Old Scots proverb